A Writing Apprenticeship

A Writing Apprenticeship

NORMAN A. BRITTIN, University of Puerto Rico

HOLT, RINEHART and WINSTON
New York   Chicago   San Francisco

FOREWORD TO THE INSTRUCTOR

This text is designed as an unpretentious, practical instrument for the teaching of composition. Many students coming to college have not read much, nor have they written much in any of their high school classes. Consequently they have very little idea of how to write English sentences according to standard patterns or how to compose solid and effective paragraphs. They are frequently set to studying material that is over their heads—material far too long and complex to serve as a model for writing. So the students often flounder around, trying to put together five hundred words on topics that are vaguely associated with the material read and which freshmen frequently are as yet too ignorant to write about. The material in this text was carefully chosen so that students would not be thrust into writing situations that are bound to be unprofitable.

As a matter of common sense, it is well to start students off by presenting paragraphs that they can use as models. There is a long and approved tradition of learning to write by imitation. But if students are really to learn by imitation, they must have models brief enough to imitate. Thus more than one third of the selections in this book contain only one paragraph; more than half of the selections contain no more than two paragraphs.

Along with the imitable model goes the practicable writing assignment. The assignments should permit the student to follow the pattern established by the paragraph. The assignments here call upon students to imitate the models on topics that are within their experience or require only direct observation of life about them.

It is hoped, too, that the very concept of apprenticeship in writing, as explained in the first pages, will produce in students a healthy, common-sense attitude toward composition. The selections in the text are examples of serious, craftsmanlike writing which in a great many respects is easily imitable by beginners. Though the names of many famous authors appear in the table of contents, the selections, which have considerable variety, do not represent the undesirable extremes of either the belletristic or the utilitarian.

The material is arranged so that it gradually becomes more complex, and the assignments naturally sometimes become longer. The selections are varied enough that the text will suit freshmen of different levels of proficiency. After a while the student should feel that he is making definite progress. By the time the student has had the experience of writing single paragraphs and linked paragraphs of the types assigned, he should have laid a really effective foundation for writing practically anything he will be called upon to write later.

The work sections accompanying the selections apply, of course, to the methods by which the authors composed their work and are designed both to make the student understand some of the standard practices in writing and to inculcate in him the habit of critical reading. As the student directs his attention closely to sentence patterns, paragraph patterns, and diction, in the way that the study questions ask him to do and that the requirement of imitation imposes upon him, he will learn a good deal about efficient reading as well as about writing. In the work sections necessary terms like "topic sentence" and "transition" are introduced along the way in such a manner that the student should become accustomed to employing them practically and naturally. The attention to diction varies with the vocabulary difficulty of the different selections; but the word-study included should help the student overcome scantiness of vocabulary and set him off on the right foot, by making him more aware of word-roots.

The text was devised with both the experienced and inexperienced instructor in mind. It is believed that the experienced instructor will feel that the strategy of this text is a sound one; it is hoped that the inexperienced instructor will find the text informative and effective.

Norman A. Brittin

Rio Piedras, Puerto Rico
December 1962

FOREWORD TO THE STUDENT

Writers and people who teach writing often call it a craft. A craft is an art or occupation that requires special skill. A person who wishes to learn a craft, whether it is pottery making, carpentry, weaving, or silversmithing, must have instruction. He must have direction and practice. Before a potter gives his apprentice a ball of clay to turn on the potter's wheel or before a carpenter puts a saw into the hand of his apprentice, he tells him to watch the master's skilled hands handle the clay, handle the saw and the board. So the apprentice tries to do exactly what the craftsman did. He tries to do it with the same smoothness and precision of his master. At first he is awkward, but as he becomes more familiar with the material used, with the tools, and with the problems that his craft has been created to solve, he gradually improves.

People who wish to learn the craft of writing go about it in the same way. They learn by imitating the work of those who are master craftsmen.

Let us remind ourselves that an apprentice is first put to making small pots, not great vessels; he is first shown how to saw boards accurately, not given a house to build. In the early stages of his apprenticeship the projects of an apprentice are small ones; only gradually do they become larger and more complicated. But after he has learned to do the little things well—after he has mastered the basic operations—he can do larger things too with success.

A student who wishes to develop his special skill in writing cannot start by composing an epic or a novel. First he must learn how to compose sentences and paragraphs. He must learn how to value words in terms of their special meanings, and he must learn how to place them in the right spots (paying attention also to the rules of grammar and syntax) so that they will form effective statements. And he must combine the sentences into paragraphs that are effective for various purposes. It has been said that if a person can write a good paragraph, he can write a book. This means, of course, that if a person has enough writing skill to compose a good paragraph, he could, if he acquired enough knowledge, create paragraph after paragraph until he had written a book.

Thus at first a carpenter's apprentice may know very little about saws, hammers, and planes, boards, planks, and nails; but after he has worked steadily with them for a few years and has learned the principles of using them, he may be in a position to build a house. Though perhaps few college freshmen will ever actually write books, they will all certainly write many other things: papers, reports, letters, speeches, articles. And if they have learned through direction and practice how to write sentences and paragraphs, they have learned the essential skills of the writing craft.

This book provides masters and models; it provides direction and practical patterns as guides. A student who does the writing assignments, always imitating the work of some master (and learning through answering questions the principles that have guided master writers), will eventually be able to produce writing that can pass inspection. He will have served his apprenticeship; and he can call himself at least a journeyman writer.

CONTENTS

III. Argument

I Description and Narration

H<small>UMAN BEINGS ARE</small> always interested in other human beings. Perhaps the majority of people are interested in people more than in anything else. Often, in conversation, one hears: "What did she look like?" "What was she wearing?" "What does he look like?" To answer such questions, we describe.

In describing, one notes the details that he has observed, or, more precisely, details that he has been made aware of by the use of all his senses—sight, hearing, taste, smell, touch. All of the environment—the world of people, the world of nature, and the man-created world—comes to one first through the senses; and if an individual is to communicate to others what his experiences in that environment are like, he must report through words what his senses have told him. Even so common an experience as washing one's face in the morning provides numerous sense impressions—the flashing on of the light in the bathroom; the gleam of chromium and porcelain; gray steam rising and clouding the mirror; the scalding feel of over-hot water; the response of the nerves to contrasting cold or lukewarm water; the smells of soap, shaving cream, and toothpaste; and the feel of the soft tubes or of the bar of soap: cold hardness if new, wet slippery smoothness if used. Nor is the ear dull to varied sounds: the splash, hiss, trickle, or gurgle of water, the rubbing of palms, popping and roaring in the ears. Maybe, because of familiarity, one pays little attention to these sense impressions—but they exist, they *are* in their totality the experience that the individual has had, and if he were to become blind, deaf, or nerve-dead, the experience would undergo radical change.

If anyone tries to answer questions about people or about environment—"What does that place look like?" "What kind of house does so-and-so live in?" "So you have been to _____! What is it like? How did you feel when you saw it? Is it pleasant? Is it scary? Is it fantastic? Is it picturesque? Is it beautiful?"—the person asked is often likely, in conversation, to give answers that are not adequate, being too hurried, too broad, too lacking in details. In writing description, however, it is possible to take time to set down details that will show with exactness just how someone looks: the person's height, shape of head, color of hair, way of gesturing or walking, shade of complexion, look of eye, twist of mouth—all these pieces of evidence can be recorded if the writer looks closely enough and if he can think of the correct terms to express them. In order to be accurate and to be interesting, he must notice details and be able to report them in abundance. But a writer must also notice telling details—that is, the particular details that give him his impressions of people and of places. A place may be awesome or dreary or uncomfortable or colorful (and a colorful place may be unpleasantly gaudy or delightfully harmonious) or spacious or crowded, and so forth. To convey the impressions that the senses have given mankind, it is essential to find words that are just right.

In the most exact meaning of the term, *description* is writing that conveys these sense impressions; but writing about people and places may also have informational purposes which are combined with description; description may lead to or be blended with character study; and description is often a necessary element in storytelling.

A large part of our lifetime goes into our associations with other people. We are constantly trying to become acquainted with them, trying to get to *know* them. Description is important in this effort, for it lets us know what sense impressions people arouse. What different pictures are conveyed by the words: "tall, dignified gentleman" and "little roly-poly fellow"! Yet, one would be more fascinated by a further report: "tall, dignified—but stupid"; "little roly-poly fellow—but sharp, even waspish!"

People are interested in surface appearances, but they are even more interested in what lies behind them. "What *kind* of person is this? What are his qualities? What are the elements of his character?" Thus persons are frequently led as they talk or write about human beings to go from description to characterization—after surveying the outward appearance, to penetrate to the inner being, the character. Of course, this calls for more knowledge, more thought, more analysis. But people are always doing it, informally as they make mental notes or chat with friends, formally as they write letters of recommendation and make other appraisals.

Though, as has been said, writing about the environment is often descriptive (it aims to make us *see* a place and sometimes to experience it with our other senses), such writing may also, at times, be as much informational as descriptive. To know that the Washington Monument is 555 feet high does not make a person see the exact look of it, but this information might be a necessary part of an article about Washington, D.C. In practice, description and informational writing, which is called exposition, often go together.

Likewise, in a story an author often tells how both places and people look; the reader generally wishes to know something about the background of the place where the story happens. Often, too, the author relates in stories how both places and people affect the feelings of other people. That is, description and storytelling (or narration) usually go together.

In the section that follows, the apprentice writer is given models for these several kinds of descriptive writing. Since everyone is in continual communication with people, it will be easy to observe them. To describe people will be one of the simplest writing exercises with which to start. And writing description will be an excellent discipline for the writing apprentice because it will begin to train his powers of observation and to show him the value of sharp, clear details. Some of the selections provide examples of characterization; some provide models for the description of places and for things seen in certain environments, such as animals. Some of the models come from stories; the section ends with readings that have more of narration than of description.

THACKERAY AS A SPEAKER
by William Cullen Bryant

1   Few expected to see so large a man: he is gigantic, six feet four at least; few expected to see so old a person; his hair appears to have kept silvery record over fifty years; and then there was a notion in the minds of many that there must be something dashing and "fast" in his appearance, whereas his costume was perfectly plain, the expression of his face grave and earnest, his address perfectly unaffected and such as we might expect to meet with in a well-bred man somewhat advanced in years. His elocution also surprised those who had derived their impressions from the English journals. His voice is a superb tenor, and possesses that pathetic tremble which is so effective in what is called emotive eloquence, while his delivery was as well suited to the communication he had to make as could well have been imagined.

2   His enunciation is perfect. Every word he uttered might have been heard in the remotest quarters of the room, yet he scarcely lifted his voice above a colloquial tone. The most striking feature in his whole manner was the utter absence of affectation of any kind. He did not permit himself to appear conscious that he was an object of peculiar interest in the audience, neither was he guilty of the greater error of not appearing to care whether they were interested or not.

Study Questions

ORGANIZATION AND CONTENT

1. Bryant stresses the points concerning Thackeray that were striking enough to impress the audience: first his height, then his age, then his appearance, and then his manner of speaking. Which one of these points receives the most space?

William Cullen Bryant, The New York *Evening Post* (1855).

2. Is there any reason for arranging these points in a particular order? Would some other order be better?
3. What details concerning Thackeray's manner of speaking does Bryant supply?

SENTENCE STRUCTURE

1. The first sentence is rather long; note that it is a balanced sentence which contrasts what people expected to experience with what they actually experienced. How many parts does the sentence have?
2. What is the key word in the first half of each part?
3. What more specific details in the second half of each part give a greater force to those key words?
4. Explain how the more specific details convey a more definite impression than the key words do.

DICTION

(The vocabulary given in this section throughout the book is taken from the text in the exact form in which it appears and in order of appearance within the article.)

1. Why does Bryant place quotation marks around *fast?*
2. Distinguish between the meanings of *elocution, eloquence,* and *enunciation.*
3. Contrast the meanings of *unaffected* and *affectation.*
4. What is the etymological connection between *eloquence* and *colloquial?*
5. Look up the meanings of *pathetic* and *emotive.* What are the roots of these words?

ASSIGNMENT

Write one solid paragraph about any person talking to a group. Describe this person, bringing out, as Bryant does, similar details of age, appearance, dress, and manner of speaking.

CHARLES BRADLAUGH
by a journalist

Mr. Bradlaugh is a tall, muscular man, who stands firm on his legs, with broad shoulders, between which is a massive, square,

The Darlington and Stockton Times (1876).

powerful head. He dresses in plain black, relieved only by an ordinary display of linen and a slender watch chain. He is closely shaven as a Roman priest. His features are large and open, his eyes are of a greyish hue, and his hair, which is fast turning grey, falls back from a brow on which intelligence, perception, and power are strongly marked. He has a face which can be very pleasing and very stern, but which conceals the emotion at will. As he sits listening to the denunciations of his opponent, the smile of incredulity, the look of astonishment, the cloud of anger, pass quickly over his countenance. Rising from his seat, and resting one hand upon the table, he commences very quietly, in a voice which, until the ear is accustomed to it, sounds unpleasant and harsh, but which, when it becomes stronger, loses much of its twang, and sounds almost musical. His enunciation is singularly distinct, not one word being lost by the audience. He addresses himself to all parts of the house—gallery as well as body. When warmed by his subject, he advances to the centre of the platform and looking his audience full in the face, and with right hand emphasising every important sentence, he expresses himself in tones so commanding and words so distinct that his hearers may be hostile or friendly, but cannot be indifferent. One may retire horrified at his sentiments, even disgusted at his irreverence and audacity—from a Christian's standpoint—but no one would go to sleep under him. He can be complimentary and humorous, but is more at home in sarcasm and denunciation. He is never ponderous; nevertheless, the grave suits him better than the gay. Cheering does not seem to affect him, though he is by no means indifferent to it, but he is quick to perceive disapproval, and is most powerful when most loudly hissed. With head erect, face coloured with a flush which has in it a little of defiance as well as earnestness, now emphasising with his right hand, now with folded arms, now joining the tips of his fingers as if to indicate the closeness of his reasoning, as he would have the audience to believe it, he stands defying opposition, even going out of his way to increase it, and revelling in his Ishmaelism.

Study Questions

ORGANIZATION AND CONTENT

1. This description of Charles Bradlaugh as a public speaker is much like the preceding description of Thackeray, but it is more detailed. More attention is given to the dress, expressions, movements, and bearing of the speaker. Point out which sentences deal with each of these topics.
2. What specific details are given in sentence 1? 2? 3? 4?
3. Explain how the details in the last sentence of the paragraph are presented so as to convey the idea of defiant vigor.

SENTENCE STRUCTURE

1. The subject of the first three sentences is the same: Mr. Bradlaugh (he)—followed by a verb. How may we say, then, that these sentences are linked to one another?
2. In sentence 4 what are the key words?
3. Note how the modifiers are arranged in sentence 4. They are adjectives, an adjective phrase, and two adjective clauses. Identify them.
4. Point out the balanced clauses in sentence 5.
5. The variety of sentences in this paragraph is noteworthy. The first five sentences all begin with independent elements. The next two sentences begin with dependent elements, the first with a dependent clause, the next with two participial phrases. How do sentences 8, 9, and 10 begin?
6. Some of the arrangements of the sentence parts within the sentences are also noteworthy: the parallel subjects, each with its adjective phrase for modifier, in sentence 6; the parallel *which*-clauses in sentence 7, and the pair of verbs making up the predicate of the second clause; the parallel main clauses in sentence 10, *he advances* and *he expresses*.

DICTION

1. The majority of words of this paragraph are simple, commonly used terms. Among them are a few less common ones, long words of Latin origin. Contrast the meanings of: *denunciation* and *enunciation, incredulity* and *astonishment.*
2. What is the etymology of *astonishment?*
3. Look up *perception, sarcasm, ponderous.*
4. *Ishmaelism* is a word made up from a proper noun, as one

might say *Daniel Boone-ism.* Find out what there was about
Ishmael that made his name suitable for the writer's purpose
here.

ASSIGNMENT

Imitate this paragraph with one about a professor, politician,
preacher, or another person addressing a group.

SHERLOCK HOLMES
by Sir Arthur Conan Doyle

1 Holmes was certainly not a difficult man to live with. He was
quiet in his ways, and his habits were regular. It was rare for him
to be up after ten at night, and he had invariably breakfasted and
gone out before I rose in the morning. Sometimes he spent his
day at the chemical laboratory, sometimes in the dissecting rooms,
and occasionally in long walks, which appeared to take him into
the lowest portions of the city. Nothing could exceed his energy
when the working fit was upon him; but now and again a
reaction would seize him, and for days on end he would lie upon
the sofa in the sitting-room, hardly uttering a word or moving
a muscle from morning to night. On these occasions I have noticed such a dreamy, vacant expression in his eyes, that I might
have suspected him of being addicted to the use of some narcotic,
had not the temperance and cleanliness of his whole life forbidden
such a notion.

2 As the weeks went by, my interest in him and my curiosity
as to his aims in life gradually deepened and increased. His very
person and appearance were such as to strike the attention of
the most casual observer. In height he was rather over six feet,
and so excessively lean that he seemed to be considerably taller.
His eyes were sharp and piercing, save during those intervals of
torpor to which I have alluded; and his thin, hawk-like nose gave
his whole expression an air of alertness and decision. His chin, too,
had the prominence and squareness which mark the man of determination. His hands were invariably blotted with ink and
stained with chemicals, yet he was possessed of extraordinary

Sir Arthur Conan Doyle, *A Study in Scarlet* (1887).

delicacy of touch, as I frequently had occasion to observe when I watched him manipulating his fragile philosophical instruments.

Study Questions

ORGANIZATION AND CONTENT

This is the first description of one of the most famous characters of modern literature—Sherlock Holmes—given shortly after Dr. Watson had met him and the two men had decided to room together. However, there are other elements here than description. These other elements make us aware of Holmes' habits and thus make us think about his character. Therefore, these paragraphs represent a combination of description and characterization. Both the description and the characterization are accomplished by means of selected details.

1. The first sentence of each paragraph is its topic sentence. The rest of each paragraph gives support to the topic sentence, or sets forth *reasons to believe that the topic sentence is true.* Give six reasons why Holmes was not a difficult man with whom to live.
2. In paragraph 2 what are the main reasons that support the idea expressed in the topic sentence?
3. Paragraph 1 is largely informational; it presents very little that we can *see.* Which details in the last two sentences allow us to form a picture in our imagination?
4. Paragraph 2 has more details that help us to form a visual image of Sherlock Holmes. Name five such details.
5. With what qualities of character has the author linked the descriptive details?
6. With these indications of Holmes' character, what terms would you use to express the kind of man that you think he is?

SENTENCE STRUCTURE

1. Point out parallel elements of sentences 2, 3, 4 of paragraph 1.
2. Sentence 5 has a semicolon. What do you think is its function?
3. The last three sentences of paragraph 2 all begin in the same way. What is the effect of these three similar beginnings?

DICTION

1. Conan Doyle's vocabulary is easy here. Perhaps it is necessary to look up *torpor, manipulating, fragile.*

2. If you can discover what *natural philosophy* is, you ought to know what *philosophical instruments* are.

ASSIGNMENT

Imitate this description in two paragraphs. In the first paragraph tell about the habits of a person; in the second, relate the appearance of the person to his character. Include at least half a dozen informational details in the first paragraph and the same number of visual details in the second.

Choose for the subject someone that you know well, such as your roommate, a laboratory partner, a member of a team, a hunting companion, or a relative.

It will probably be useful, *before writing* the paragraphs, to make lists of the details that give life to the subject and fullness to the paragraphs.

DICK HUMBIRD
by F. Scott Fitzgerald

1   Dick Humbird had, ever since freshman year, seemed to Amory a perfect type of aristocrat. He was slender but well-built —black curly hair, straight features, and rather a dark skin. Everything he said sounded intangibly appropriate. He possessed infinite courage, an averagely good mind, and a sense of honor with a clear charm and noblesse oblige that varied it from righteousness. He could dissipate without going to pieces, and even his most bohemian adventures never seemed "running it out." People dressed like him, tried to talk as he did. . . . Amory decided that he probably held the world back, but he wouldn't have changed him. . . .

2   He differed from the healthy type that was essentially middle-class—he never seemed to perspire. Some people couldn't be familiar with a chauffeur without having it returned; Humbird could have lunched at Sherry's with a colored man, yet people would have somehow known that it was all right. He was not a snob, though he knew only half his class. His friends ranged from

the highest to the lowest, but it was impossible to "cultivate" him. Servants worshipped him, and treated him like a god. He seemed the eternal example of what the upper class tries to be.

Study Questions

ORGANIZATION AND CONTENT

1. What topic idea is the author trying to support or "prove" in these two paragraphs?
2. What is the topic sentence of paragraph 1? Of paragraph 2?
3. How much of the material is allotted to visual details?
4. What does the rest of the material consist of?
5. The characterization of Dick Humbird is seen through Amory's eyes—or presents the conclusions Amory has drawn after he has observed the behavior of Dick Humbird. Some of the material is quite abstract (look up *abstract*)—sentence 4, for example. Explain the differences in the manner of presenting Dick Humbird in sentences 2, 3, 4, 5, and 6.

SENTENCE STRUCTURE

1. Note that in paragraph 2 the sentences are largely set up in terms of contrasts. Explain how the contrasts are expressed in sentences 1, 2, 3, and 4.
2. What is the main contrast that governs these sentences?
3. Why did Fitzgerald use ellipsis periods after the last two sentences of paragraph 1?
4. One sentence contains a semicolon. Why?

DICTION

1. What are the roots of *intangibly* and *dissipate?*
2. Point out the abstract terms in paragraph 1, sentence 4.
3. Fitzgerald placed quotation marks around "running it out" and "cultivate." What is the function of these quotation marks?
4. Look up *noblesse oblige.* Should it have been italicized? Should *chauffeur* have been?
5. Explain the differences between an aristocrat, a bohemian, and a snob.

ASSIGNMENT

Write a character analysis of a person who seems to represent some type of individual, such as the snob, the bohemian, the middle-class or working-class person, the ambitious student, the social climber, the sincerely pious person, the pious hypocrite. Use only a little description but much illustration of the person's behavior plus an interpretation of his actions. Part of the problem will be to arrange the material in one unified paragraph or in two paragraphs, as Fitzgerald does, with each paragraph containing an unmistakable topic sentence.

MRS. JACK GARDNER
by Cleveland Amory

1   For a Boston Society which has never lacked for grandes dames to have to admit that its greatest was not a Bostonian at all but a New York import is a stern story indeed. Furthermore this greatest of grandes dames was a lady who persisted in regarding herself as a sort of dedicated spirit to wake up Boston. The daughter of a New York dry-goods merchant named David Stewart, she was christened Isabella. In the year 1860 she married John Lowell Gardner, son of the last of Boston's East India merchants, and moved to Boston. From then until her death in 1924 at the age of eighty-five Isabella Stewart Gardner proceeded to do everything that Proper Boston women do not do, and then some. "In a Society," wrote Lucius Beebe, "where entertaining Major Higginson at tea and sleigh-riding on the Brighton Road on Sunday afternoon were the ultimate public activities endorsed by decorum, she soon became far from anonymous."

2   Mrs. Gardner didn't drink tea; she drank beer. She adored it, she said. She didn't go sleigh-riding; instead, she went walking down Tremont Street with a lion named Rex on a leash. She gave at-homes at her Beacon Street house and received her guests from a perch in the lower branches of a mimosa tree. Told that "everybody in Boston" was either a Unitarian or an Episcopalian, she became a Buddhist; then when the pleasure of that shock had worn off she became such a High-Church Episcopalian that her religion differed from Catholicism only in respect to allegiance

to the Pope. Advised that the best people in Boston belonged to clubs she formed one of her own named the "It" Club. In Boston one coachman was enough for anybody. But Mrs. Gardner soon showed she wasn't anybody. She kept two footmen as well as a coachman and rarely drove out in her carriage without all three of them in full livery. Warned that a woman's social position in Boston might be judged in inverse ratio to her appearance, she spent thousands of dollars a year on the latest Paris fashions. She saw Cabots and Lowells leave their jewels in their safe-deposit boxes; she picked out her two largest diamonds, had them set on gold wire springs and wore them waving some six inches above her hair like the antennae of a butterfly. Mrs. Gardner even told risqué stories and told them in mixed company—at the same time, her bout with Buddhism behind her, each Lent with much fanfare she piously atoned for her misdeeds by scrubbing the steps of the Church of the Advent and sending out black-bordered invitations to Holy Communion.

³ Hypnotic was the word for this woman. She had a way with her. Plain of face to the point of homeliness and short of stature, she had a strikingly curvaceous figure and attracted artists by the score, most of whom offered to paint her merely for the pleasure of doing so. When she finally chose John Singer Sargent to do her portrait, she once more showed her scorn for Bostonian propriety by having him paint her in a black low-necked dress with a rope of pearls around her waist and a black shawl drawn tightly around her hips. Exhibited at the gentlemanly St. Botolph Club in the winter of 1888–89 the picture caused so much comment that her husband had it removed and declared it would never be exhibited again as long as he lived. So far as it is known this is the only occasion he or anyone else ever told Mrs. Gardner what to do. "To dominate others," writes her biographer and present-day executor, Morris Carter, "gave Mrs. Gardner such pleasure that she must have regretted the passing of slavery."

Study Questions

ORGANIZATION AND CONTENT

1. What is the main theme that continues throughout this account of the famous Mrs. Gardner?
2. Paragraph 2 does not have any general statement to serve as a topic sentence. What idea would cover the many details mentioned in paragraph 2?
3. What relation does paragraph 2 have to paragraph 1?
4. How does the principal thought of paragraph 3 contrast with that of paragraph 2?

SENTENCE STRUCTURE

1. Note that the author begins many of his sentences with dependent phrases or clauses. He uses the participial modifier like the "Told that 'everybody in Boston' . . ." in paragraph 2, the appositive as in "The daughter of a New York dry-goods merchant . . ." in paragraph 1, the adjective plus modifiers in the "Plain of face to the point of homeliness . . ." in paragraph 3, and a series of prepositional phrases in the "From then until her death . . ." in paragraph 1. Does he overdo the opening with dependent elements?
2. However, the first several sentences of paragraph 2 are of a different type. Explain what their difference is.
3. What is the effect of this "change of pace" in the early part of paragraph 2?
4. To what extent would you say that Amory has achieved variety in his sentence style in these paragraphs?

DICTION

1. Look up *grandes dames, ultimate, decorum, livery, risqué, fanfare, atoned, propriety.*
2. What are the chief differences among the beliefs of Unitarians, Episcopalians, and Buddhists?
3. Comment on the effect of these terms: *and then some, bout, curvaceous.*

ASSIGNMENT

Write two or three paragraphs about an unconventional person. To do justice to your model, Mrs. Jack Gardner, choose the most unconventional person you have ever known, one who has seemed "wild" and who has delighted in challenging social conventions wherever he or she has lived.

Note that though there is some description here, the author places most stress upon Mrs. Gardner's activities and personality. He does not say much about her character or temperament. Sentence 2 of paragraph 1 gives necessary information in this respect and so does the last sentence of paragraph 3. Paragraph 2 is devoted entirely to the actions of Mrs. Gardner. Do the same in your paragraphs; an honest report of facts is generally very effective.

NAPOLEON
by *Varnhagen von Else* (*Thomas Carlyle, trans.*)

1   "We had driven to the Tuileries, and arrived through a great press of guards and people at a chamber, of which I had already heard, under the name of *Salle des Ambassadeurs*. The way in which, here in this narrow ill-furnished pen, so many high personages stood jammed together, had something ludicrous and insulting in it, and was indeed the material of many a Paris jest.— The richest uniforms and court-dresses were, with difficulty and anxiety, struggling hitherward and thitherward; intermixed with Imperial liveries of men handing refreshments, who always, by the near peril, suspended every motion of those about them. The talk was loud and vivacious on all sides; people seeking acquaintances, seeking more room, seeking better light. Seriousness of mood, and dignified concentration of oneself, seemed foreign to all; and what a man could not bring with him, there was nothing here to produce. The whole matter had a distressful, offensive air; you found yourself ill-off, and waited out of humor. My look, however, dwelt with especial pleasure on the members of our Austrian Embassy, whose bearing and demeanor did not discredit the dignity of the old Imperial house.—Prince Schwartzenberg, in particular, had a stately aspect; ease without negligence, gravity without assumption, and over all an honest goodness of expression; beautifully contrasted with the smirking saloon-

Thomas Carlyle, "Varnhagen von Else's Memoirs," in *Critical and Miscellaneous Essays* (Boston, 1885).

activity, the perked-up courtierism and pretentious nullity of many here. . . .

2   "At last the time came for going up to audience. On the first announcement of it, all rushed without order towards the door; you squeezed along, you pushed and shoved your neighbor without ceremony. Chamberlains, pages and guards filled the passages and antechamber; restless, overdone officiousness struck you here too; the soldiers seemed the only figures that knew how to behave in their business,—and this, truly, they had learned, not at Court, but from their drill-sergeants.

3   "We had formed ourselves into a half-circle in the Audience Hall, and got placed in several crowded ranks, when the cry of '*L'Empereur!*' announced the appearance of Napoleon, who entered from the lower side of the apartment. In simple blue uniform, his little hat under his arm, he walked heavily towards us. His bearing seemed to me to express the contradiction between a will that would attain something, and a contempt for those by whom it was to be attained. An imposing appearance he would undoubtedly have liked to have; and yet it seemed to him not worth the trouble of acquiring; acquiring, I may say, for by nature he certainly had it not. Thus there alternated in his manner a negligence and a studiedness, which combined themselves only in unrest and dissatisfaction. He turned first to the Austrian Embassy, which occupied one extremity of the half-circle. The consequences of the unlucky festival gave occasion to various questions and remarks. The Emperor sought to appear sympathetic, he even used words of emotion; but this tone by no means succeeded with him, and accordingly he soon let it drop. To the Russian Ambassador, Kurakin, who stood next, his manner had already changed into a rougher; and in his farther progress some face or some thought must have stung him, for he got into violent anger; broke stormfully out on some one or other, not of the most important there, whose name has now escaped me; could be pacified with no answer, but demanded always new; rated and threatened, and held the poor man, for a good space, in tormenting annihilation. Those who stood nearer, and were looking at this scene, not without anxieties of their own, declared afterwards that there was no cause at all for such fury; that the Emperor had merely been seeking an opportunity to vent his ill-humor, and had done

so even intentionally, on this poor wight, that all the rest might
be thrown into due terror, and every opposition beforehand
beaten down.

4   "As he walked on, he again endeavored to speak more
mildly; but his jarred humor still sounded through. His words
were short, hasty, as if shot from him, and on the most indifferent
matters had a passionate rapidity; nay, when he wished to be
kindly, it still sounded as if he were in anger. Such a raspy, un-
tamed voice as that of his I have hardly heard.

5   "His eyes were dark, overclouded, fixed on the ground before him; and only glanced backwards in side-looks now and then,
swift and sharp, on the persons there. When he smiled, it was
but the mouth and a part of the cheeks that smiled; brow and
eyes remained gloomily motionless. If he constrained these also,
as I have subsequently seen him do, his countenance took a
still more distorted expression. This union of gloom and smile
had something frightfully repulsive in it. I know not what to
think of the people who have called this countenance gracious,
and its kindliness attractive. Were not his features, though un-
deniably beautiful in the plastic sense, yet hard and rigorous like
marble; foreign to all trust, incapable of any heartiness?"

Study Questions

ORGANIZATION AND CONTENT

1. These five paragraphs reveal the impressions made on an observer by a famous man—Napoleon—and the opinions that the
   observer formed as he watched the famous man among the
   crowd that attended him. Were the impressions and the opinions chiefly favorable or unfavorable?
2. What principle governs the order in which the paragraphs are
   presented?
3. What point is the author making in paragraph 1 with his remarks on the Austrian Embassy and Prince Schwartzenberg?
4. Why are paragraphs 2 and 4 shorter than the others?
5. In dealing with his problem of writing description and characterization the author tries to make the reader see the man, and
   he also expresses his own opinions. How many details in the
   last three paragraphs are visual?

6. How many terms in the last three paragraphs express the author's opinion of the subject?

SENTENCE STRUCTURE

1. The majority of the sentences are long rather than short. Pick out the half-dozen shortest sentences.
2. Does each short sentence, when it appears, have any particular effect in the paragraph?
3. For what purposes does the author use semicolons in his sentences?

DICTION

1. Paragraphs 1 and 2 tell of the crowd at the Tuileries before Napoleon made his appearance. Make a list of the details in these paragraphs that convey unfavorable impressions.
2. The author has used a dozen or more phrases or terms in these paragraphs that show how he felt. Which of these terms would you select as the most effective?
3. Which ones are nouns? adjectives? verbs?
4. Napoleon appears in paragraph 3. Which terms here do the most to convey the impression which he made upon the author? Note the terms which contrast with one another.
5. How large a proportion of adjectives does the author use in the last three paragraphs?
6. Which adjectives have the greatest effect in expressing the feelings and opinions of the author?
7. Look up *Tuileries, ludicrous, vivacious, demeanor, smirking, courtierism, pretentious, nullity, officiousness, studiedness, rated, annihilation, wight, constrained, distorted, plastic, rigorous.*
8. Learn the roots of *ludicrous, vivacious, nullity, annihilation, distorted.*

ASSIGNMENT

In imitation of the account of Napoleon write from three to five paragraphs describing and characterizing someone of whom you disapprove or whose behavior has disappointed you. Show this person among a group of people, as at a reception, dance, meeting, rehearsal, or party of some kind. Be sure to choose carefully the words that will express strongly, and exactly, how you feel.

FOX HOW
by Mrs. Humphry Ward

The gray-stone house stands now, as it stood then, on a "how" or rising ground in the beautiful Westmorland valley leading from Ambleside to Rydal. The "Doctor" built it as a holiday paradise for himself and his children, in the year 1833. It is a modest building, with ten bedrooms and three sitting-rooms. Its windows look straight into the heart of Fairfield, the beautiful semicircular mountain which rears its hollowed front and buttressing scaurs against the north, far above the green floor of the valley. That the house looked north never troubled my grandfather or his children. What they cared for was the perfect outline of the mountain wall, the "pensive glooms," hovering in that deep breast of Fairfield, the magic never-ending chase of sunlight and cloud across it on fine days, and the beauty of the soft woodland clothing its base. The garden was his children's joy as it became mine. Its little beck with its mimic bridges, its encircling river, its rocky knolls, its wild strawberries and wild raspberries, its queen of birch-trees rearing a stately head against the distant mountain, its rhododendrons growing like weeds on its mossy banks, its velvet turf, and long silky grass in the parts left wild—all these things have made the joy of three generations.

Study Questions

ORGANIZATION AND CONTENT

1. The author of this paragraph is remembering a house that she knew as a child. The paragraph is partly explanatory but mostly descriptive. Is its emphasis mainly on the setting of the house, or on the house itself?
2. After the first three sentences, which are informational, what element concerning the house is brought out?
3. Sentence 6 mentions four specific details. What are they?
4. The last sentence contains mention of eight details. These details all relate to what?

From *A Writer's Recollections* by Mrs. Humphry Ward. Copyright 1918. Reprinted by permission of Harper & Row, Publishers.

SENTENCE STRUCTURE

1. Indicate all the words in the first five sentences that mean *house*. These words link the five sentences together; the reader can pass easily from one to the next.
2. What word in sentence 6 is picked up in sentences 7 and 8 to provide links among these three sentences?
3. How does the position of the list of details in sentence 8 differ from that of the details in sentence 6?

DICTION

1. Mrs. Ward's vocabulary is easy here. Look up *buttressing, scaurs, beck*. What terms would an American writer have been likely to use instead of *scaurs* and *beck?*
2. What words in the description would justify the idea of "paradise" which is mentioned in sentence 2?
3. Mrs. Ward often uses terms which suggest that the thing she is writing about is something else, or is like something else: "paradise," for example, in sentence 2. Her language is "figurative"; that is, she uses metaphors and similes. Consider the figurative use of: *heart, rears, buttressing, floor, chase, clothing, mimic, queen, growing like weeds, velvet, silky*. To express her feeling about Fox How, how much has the author relied on these figurative terms?
4. Since description has to do with the effects of things on our human senses—sight, smell, hearing, taste, touch—such figurative terms often have extra value for the descriptive writer. To which of the senses do the terms listed above make an appeal?

ASSIGNMENT

Imitate this paragraph with a paragraph about a building that you know. Select a building with a striking or interesting setting, begin with some information about the building, and then describe its setting. Pay particular attention to the adjectives that you use, as Mrs. Ward does in the second half of her paragraph. In the final sentence list from six to ten details, as she does, with a summarizing statement at the end, after a dash.

A BEDROOM
by Charles Dickens

They mounted up and up, through the musty smell of an old close house, little used, to a large garret bed-room. Meagre and spare, like all the other rooms, it was even uglier and grimmer than the rest, by being the place of banishment for the worn out furniture. Its movables were ugly old chairs with worn out seats, and ugly old chairs without any seats; a thread-bare patternless carpet, a maimed table, a crippled wardrobe, a lean set of fire-irons like the skeleton of a set deceased, a washing stand that looked as if it had stood for ages in a hail of dirty soap-suds, and a bedstead with four bare atomies of posts, each terminating in a spike, as if for the dismal accommodation of lodgers who might prefer to impale themselves. Arthur opened the long low window, and looked out upon the old blasted and blackened forest of chimneys, and the old red glare in the sky which had seemed to him once upon a time but a nightly reflection of the fiery environment that was presented to his childish fancy in all directions, let it look where it would.

Study Questions

ORGANIZATION AND CONTENT

1. This paragraph has four sentences. Explain exactly what the purpose of each sentence is.
2. Explain what made Dickens place the sentences in the order that they are in.

SENTENCE STRUCTURE

1. Why is sentence 1 the shortest of the four sentences?
2. How does the organization of sentence 2 differ from that of sentence 1?
3. What is the main clause of each sentence? What is the position of the modifiers in relation to each main clause? (That is, what principles of *sentence management* has Dickens used?)
4. Explain how Dickens has connected the four sentences so that the paragraph has unity.

Charles Dickens, *Little Dorrit* (1855–1857).

1. The vocabulary is simple. You probably know the meanings of all the terms used, except *atomies;* but it might be helpful to look up some of the words, nevertheless, so that you may have a sharper idea of their connotations—and perhaps denotations too. (You may need to look up *connotation* and *denotation.*)
2. In this description of a bedroom Dickens chooses words to create an impression of a displeasing or unpleasant place. What is there about the room that makes this unpleasant impression upon Arthur, the man who has entered it after many years? Make a list of the words that suggest something distasteful or unpleasant. Are they mainly nouns, adjectives, verbs, or adverbs?
3. What words are the key words of the description? Which words has Dickens emphasized by repeating them?
4. The word *meagre* appears in sentence 2. What other words have the same sort of suggestion as *meagre* and thus contribute to a harmonious impression of something displeasing?
5. Dickens has used language in a figurative way here. Explain the figurative use of: *spare, banishment, maimed, crippled, lean, hail, forest.*
6. What connotations do these terms have? What other words have a special connotative value?
7. Contrast the impressions made by this description with the impressions conveyed by the vocabulary of Mrs. Ward's description of Fox How.

ASSIGNMENT

Imitate this paragraph with one describing a room and conveying a single impression. Be sure to include ten or a dozen details, as Dickens does. Use striking adjectives. Use some terms in a figurative way. You might take your own room; a living room prepared for a party, just before the guests arrive; the same room just after the party is over; a living room when you enter it at two o'clock in the morning; a store, an office, or a shack.

THE MAIN ROOM OF AN INN
by Sir Arthur Conan Doyle

The room was not unlike a stable. The low ceiling, smoke-blackened and dingy, was pierced by several square trap-doors with rough-hewn ladders leading up to them. The walls of bare unpainted planks were studded here and there with great wooden pins, placed at irregular intervals and heights, from which hung overtunics, wallets, whips, bridles, and saddles. Over the fireplace were suspended six or seven shields of wood, with coats-of-arms rudely daubed upon them, which showed by their varying degrees of smokiness and dirt that they had been placed there at different periods. There was no furniture, save a single long dresser covered with coarse crockery, and a number of wooden benches and trestles, the legs of which sank deeply into the soft clay floor, while the only light, save that of the fire, was furnished by three torches stuck in sockets on the wall, which flickered and crackled, giving forth a strong resinous odor. All this was novel and strange to the cloister-bred youth; but most interesting of all was the motley circle of guests who sat eating their collops round the blaze. They were a humble group of wayfarers, such as might have been found that night in any inn through the length and breadth of England; but to him they represented that vague world against which he had been so frequently and so earnestly warned. It did not seem to him, from what he could see of it, to be such a very wicked place after all.

Study Questions

ORGANIZATION AND CONTENT

1. In this paragraph an observer who has never traveled before is looking upon a scene that is new to him—the main room of a medieval inn. The author describes what the observer sees from his seat in a corner. This is his unchanging *point of view*. Would any of the material be differently presented, or omitted, if his point of view were changed?

Sir Arthur Conan Doyle, *The White Company* (New York, Harper & Brothers, 1894).

2. The dominant impression is stated in sentence 1. What items support this impression?
3. At what point in the paragraph are people introduced? Where does the writer mention the impression that they make upon the observer?
4. What would be lost from the total effect if there were no other guests in the room?

SENTENCE STRUCTURE

1. A general principle of good writing is that modifiers should be as close as possible to the words they modify. Note that in several sentences the author has tucked away modifiers, placing them just after the words they modify—a pair of adjectives in sentence 2, for example. Point out examples of the same technique in other sentences.
2. Both sentence 6 and sentence 7 are balanced with a *but* in the middle. We might say that the semicolon before the *but* in each sentence serves as a fulcrum. Semicolons are frequently used in this way; they are effective in such sentences. And *but* is an important word in English. What is its meaning when it is used in a sentence thus?

DICTION

1. A few words here are unusual. Look up *dresser* in the British sense. What word would an American writer probably have used instead?
2. Look up *motley, collops, cloister-bred*. Pay special attention to the etymology of *cloister*. The word is important in this instance for its suggestions concerning the way in which the observer responds to the scene before him.
3. Certain details which suggest that the place was unrefined are mentioned in sentence 2 and sentence 3. There adjectives particularly express a feeling of unrefinement. Which words in these sentences are the most effective in this respect?
4. What adjectives of other sentences support the impression of unrefinement?

ASSIGNMENT

Describe a room from one point of view. It might be a classroom with just a few persons in it, a professor's office, a printing shop, a hunter's cabin, a poolroom, a restaurant, a dance hall, or a beer joint. Be sure to survey the room and give a clear account of the details to be seen—the furniture, what is on the walls, and so forth. State the dominant impression in your first sentence. Select adjectives that will support this dominant impression.

THE TROIS COURONNES HOTEL
by Henry James

At the little town of Vevay, in Switzerland, there is a particularly comfortable hotel. Here are, indeed, many hotels; for the entertainment of tourists is the business of the place, which, as many travellers will remember, is seated upon the edge of a remarkably blue lake—a lake that it behooves every tourist to visit. The shore of the lake presents an unbroken array of establishments of this order, of every category, from the "grand hotel" of the newest fashion, with a chalk-white front, a hundred balconies, and a dozen flags flying from its roof, to the little Swiss *pension* of an elder day, with its name inscribed in German-looking lettering upon a pink or yellow wall, and an awkward summer-house in the angle of the garden. One of the hotels at Vevay, however, is famous, even classical, being distinguished from any of its upstart neighbors by an air both of luxury and of maturity. In this region, in the month of June, American travellers are extremely numerous; it may be said, indeed, that Vevay assumes at this period some of the characteristics of an American watering-place. There are sights and sounds which evoke a vision, an echo, of Newport and Saratoga. There is a flitting hither and thither of "stylish" young girls, a rustling of muslin flounces, a rattle of dance-music in the morning hours, a sound of high-pitched voices at all times. You receive an impression of these things at the excellent inn of the Trois Couronnes, and are transported in fancy to the Ocean House or to Congress Hall. But at the Trois Couronnes, it must be added, there are other features that are much at variance with these suggestions: neat German waiters, who look like secretaries of legation, Russian princesses sitting in the garden; little Polish boys walking about, held by the hand, with their governors; a view of the sunny crest of the Dent du Midi and the picturesque towers of the Castle of Chillon.

Henry James, *Daisy Miller* (1879).

Study Questions

ORGANIZATION AND CONTENT

1. This paragraph not only describes but gives information. We might call it an example of expository description. Point out the terms: (a) that cause the reader to see; (b) that cause him to understand.
2. What are the most significant points about the hotel?
3. The author makes use of comparison and contrast. How does this hotel compare with other hotels in the town? In what ways might it remind an American visitor of an American hotel? In what ways is it different from an American hotel?

SENTENCE STRUCTURE

1. One of the things to be noted about sentence management in this selection is the use of "interrupters"—terms that are set off by commas, such as *indeed* in sentence 2. Point out other words, phrases, and clauses that are set off in this way within the other sentences.
2. Note how the details are listed in sentence 7 and the last sentence. Explain the functions of the marks of punctuation used in those two sentences.

DICTION

1. Look up *category, pension, classical, evoke, picturesque.*
2. Which words are especially effective in the sentence that begins "There is a flitting . . ."?

ASSIGNMENT

Begin your paragraph in the same way: "In the little town of . . ." or "In the city of . . . ," and concentrate on one building among several of the same sort—a fraternity house, an old mansion, an office building, a bank, a college building, a motel. Describe this building at a time when it is full of activity. Include contrast and comparison, and indicate what impression the building makes upon the observer.

VIEW FROM ROCHESTER BRIDGE
by Charles Dickens

1   Bright and pleasant was the sky, balmy the air, and beautiful the appearance of every object around, as Mr. Pickwick leant over the balustrades of Rochester Bridge, contemplating nature, and waiting for breakfast. The scene was indeed one which might well have charmed a far less reflective mind, than that to which it was presented.

2   On the left of the spectator lay the ruined wall, broken in many places, and in some, overhanging the narrow beach below in rude and heavy masses. Huge knots of sea-weed hung upon the jagged and pointed stones, trembling in every breath of wind; and the green ivy clung mournfully round the dark and ruined battlements. Behind it rose the ancient castle, its towers roofless, and its massive walls crumbling away, but telling us proudly of its own might and strength, as when, seven hundred years ago, it rang with the clash of arms, or resounded with the noise of feasting and revelry. On either side, the banks of the Medway, covered with cornfields and pastures, with here and there a windmill, or a distant church, stretched away as far as the eye could see, presenting a rich and varied landscape, rendered more beautiful by the changing shadows which passed swiftly across it, as the thin and half-formed clouds skimmed away in the light of the morning sun. The river, reflecting the clear blue of the sky, glistened and sparkled as it flowed noiselessly on; and the oars of the fishermen dipped into the water with a clear and liquid sound, as the heavy but picturesque boats glided slowly down the stream.

Study Questions

ORGANIZATION AND CONTENT

1. In the first paragraph what are we told about who the observer is, the place from which he is observing, the time of day, and the quality of the scene?
2. Paragraph 2 is description proper. The scene, we are told, has

Charles Dickens, *The Posthumous Papers of the Pickwick Club,* better known as *The Pickwick Papers* (1836–1837).

"charm," and it would appear that Dickens means the romantic charm that appealed to early nineteenth-century readers. Would it be fair to say that Dickens' description is somewhat tritely romantic? Why?

3. Dickens includes a considerable number of details though they are not viewed very closely. In describing the scene, Dickens was handling a problem of perspective in description (one would expect that more attention should be given to the nearer objects, less attention to those more distant). Indicate how Dickens dealt with this problem.

SENTENCE STRUCTURE

1. Dickens has certain mannerisms. Note the way in which sentence 1 opens, the parallel phrasing, and the many alliterative words. How many words in sentence 1 begin with *b?*
2. Note in paragraph 2 the many pairs of adjectives connected with *and*, like "rude and heavy." How many others are there?
3. The sentences are rather long. Do they flow smoothly or not?

DICTION

1. What are the connotations of such terms as "clung mournfully," "dark and ruined battlements," "massive walls," "might and strength," "feasting and revelry," "as far as the eye could see," "thin and half-formed clouds skimmed away," "clear and liquid sound"?
2. Which of these terms seem the most trite? The least trite?
3. Make a list of the nouns indicating the things that Mr. Pickwick saw from the bridge.
4. How many adjectives does Dickens use in this passage? How many verbs?
5. Which are the most effective verbs and adjectives?

ASSIGNMENT

The view that Mr. Pickwick saw was given definite limits because he was standing on a bridge looking up a river. In the same way give a person a particular site from which to observe, and describe in one or two paragraphs the view that he sees. You may place him on a bridge, as Dickens did; on a high place in a highway or a country lane so that he can look off down the road; at a town or city square that he can look across; on a wharf; in a railway yard; or at the gate of a factory. Include at least a dozen specific details, some nearby and others farther away.

ANIMALS ON THE WESTERN PLAINS
by Francis Parkman

But in the meantime my ride had been by no means a solitary one. The face of the country was dotted far and wide with countless hundreds of buffalo. They trooped along in files and columns, bulls, cows, and calves, on the green faces of the declivities in front. They scrambled away over the hills to the right and left; and far off, the pale blue swells in the extreme distance were dotted with innumerable specks. Sometimes I surprised shaggy old bulls grazing alone, or sleeping behind the ridges I ascended. They would leap up at my approach, stare stupidly at me through their tangled manes, and then gallop heavily away. The antelope were very numerous; and as they are always bold when in the neighborhood of buffalo, they would approach to look at me, gaze intently with their great round eyes, then suddenly leap aside, and stretch lightly away over the prairie, as swiftly as a race-horse. Squalid, ruffian-like wolves sneaked through the hollows and sandy ravines. Several times I passed through villages of prairie-dogs, who sat, each at the mouth of his burrow, holding his paws before him in a supplicating attitude, and yelping away most vehemently, whisking his little tail with every squeaking cry he uttered. Prairie-dogs are not fastidious in their choice of companions; various long checkered snakes were sunning themselves in the midst of the village, and demure little gray owls, with a large white ring around each eye, were perched side by side with the rightful inhabitants. The prairie teemed with life. Again and again I looked toward the crowded hill-sides, and was sure I saw horsemen; and riding near, with a mixture of hope and dread, for Indians were abroad, I found them transformed into a group of buffalo. There was nothing in human shape amid all this vast congregation of brute forms.

Study Questions

ORGANIZATION AND CONTENT

1. Francis Parkman tells in this paragraph of the animals he saw while riding on the Western plains in 1846. The point of view

Francis Parkman, *The California and Oregon Trail* (1849).

is quite different from the station of Mr. Pickwick in the previous selection. Explain why.

2. Though Parkman was alone and temporarily lost, his ride was certainly not "a solitary one"! How many different kinds of animals does he mention?
3. Of what significance is the last sentence?

SENTENCE STRUCTURE

1. How many of Parkman's sentences start with a subject-verb construction? How many have some sort of modifier before the subject?
2. Do any of the sentences begin with a dependent clause?
3. What is the effect of having a majority of sentences constructed like Parkman's?

DICTION

1. Notice that Parkman describes the characteristic movements of animals. He does this by means of carefully chosen verbs. Count the verbs in the paragraph. Which three verbs have the greatest force?
2. This paragraph makes an extremely strong appeal to the eye— to the sense of sight. However, not all of this appeal comes from verbs. What details expressed by means of nouns and adjectives appeal to the eye?
3. Look up *declivities, supplicating, vehemently, demure, teemed, congregation, squalid.*
4. What is the effect of mentioning the "squalid, ruffian-like wolves" between the antelope and the prairie-dogs? What is the connotation of *squalid?*

ASSIGNMENT

Few people today could have the same experience that Parkman had. But one should be able to create a similar paragraph with a moving point of view based on city sights or on movements of things observed during a windy day. At certain seasons almost anyone could write such a paragraph describing birds rather than animals. In your paragraph use sharp, precise verbs to convey the exact look of the movements you describe.

HERDING BUFFALO IN INDIA
by Rudyard Kipling

Then Mowgli picked out a shady place, and lay down and slept while the buffaloes grazed round him. Herding in India is one of the laziest things in the world. The cattle move and crunch, and lie down, and move on again, and they do not even low. They only grunt, and the buffaloes very seldom say anything, but get down into the muddy pools one after another, and work their way into the mud till only their noses and staring china-blue eyes show above the surface, and there they lie like logs. The sun makes the rocks dance in the heat, and the herd-children hear one kite (never any more) whistling almost out of sight overhead, and they know that if they died, or a cow died, that kite would sweep down, and the next kite miles away would see him drop and would follow, and the next, and the next, and almost before they were dead there would be a score of hungry kites come out of nowhere. Then they sleep and wake and sleep again, and weave little baskets of dried grass and put grasshoppers in them; or catch two praying-mantises and make them fight; or string a necklace of red and black jungle-nuts; or watch a lizard basking on a rock, or a snake hunting a frog near the wallows. Then they sing long, long songs with odd native quavers at the end of them, and the day seems longer than most people's whole lives, and perhaps they make a mud castle with mud figures of men and horses and buffaloes, and put reeds into the men's hands, and pretend that they are kings and the figures are their armies, or that they are gods to be worshipped. Then evening comes, and the children call, and the buffaloes lumber up out of the sticky mud with noises like gunshots going off one after the other, and they all string across the gray plain back to the twinkling village lights.

Study Questions

ORGANIZATION AND CONTENT

1. Kipling's paragraph tells about a certain customary activity in the out-of-doors: herding buffalo in India. What are the main subtopics that are dealt with in the paragraph?

Rudyard Kipling, "Tiger, Tiger!" in *The Jungle Book* (1894).

2. What things do the herders see? hear? do?
3. Is this paragraph rich in details or not? Explain.
4. Why does the day of the herders seem long and tedious?

SENTENCE STRUCTURE

1. Notice that Kipling's sentences contain many coordinating conjunctions. Mark the coordinating conjunctions in sentences 3 through 7.
2. Which is the longest sentence of the paragraph?
3. What is the effect of lengthening sentences with many coordinating conjunctions?

DICTION

1. Count the verbs in the paragraph. Is the number large or small?
2. Make a list of the verbs. How do these verbs compare, for precision and vigor, with those of Parkman in the preceding reading?
3. Which are the most effective of Kipling's adjectives?

ASSIGNMENT

Write a similar paragraph about herding in an American scene, or about the succession of things experienced while hunting, or about trying to make the time pass anywhere when one is a bored child. Or you might achieve the same effect of monotony plus activity by telling about the day of a convalescent or about the evening of a babysitter. Cram your paragraph with details, and stress verbs!

YOUNG KING PENGUINS
by Robert Cushman Murphy

[1]   Newly hatched King Penguins seem never to have been carefully described. The youngest I have seen were taken in early June at South Georgia, and were presumably two or more months of age. The smallest specimen is 50 centimeters in length. Its bill, to which the egg-tooth still adheres, measures only 49 millimeters from the gape. As among most long-beaked birds, the differential spurt in the growth of the bill begins in later youth. The down in the June specimens is of a nearly uniform dusky or smoky drab color all over the body. In the youngest it is thin and short over a mask-like area on the face. Traces of light-colored natal down still cling to the tips of the juvenal down on the head. The Mask, at least, is suggestive of the young Emperor Penguin.

[2]   The partly grown chicks of the King Penguin toddle about after their parents when the latter are on the move. They chirp and whistle, endeavor to nibble at the bills of the old birds, and sometimes plead by swaying the head to and fro in the manner of a young cormorant. When the adult has been sufficiently stimulated, it regurgitates food into its gullet, lowers its head, and the chick dives in up to the shoulders.

[3]   The young ones are mutually congenial, curious, and entirely without fear of man. If you remain among a band of them, they are likely to crowd about and squeak as though they expected to be fed. Such groups reminded me of college students wearing raccoon-skin coats. Buller likened them to "retriever pups," but the aptest fanciful name ever applied was that of sealers at the Crozet Islands, who dubbed them "oakum-boys." They look exactly like large handfuls of oakum ready for calking the seams of a ship. The long woolly down affords an excellent nonconductive winter covering, but by springtime (November) it is liable to be uncomfortably warm during sunny hours. Chicks that have not begun to shed sometimes sit and pant with wide-open bills as if in distress.

Robert Cushman Murphy, *Oceanic Birds of South America* (New York, The Macmillan Company, 1936). Reprinted with permission of The American Museum of Natural History.

⁴ Yearling birds, such as I saw in December, may have body down 90 millimeters or more in length. It fades with age, turning a streaky golden brown or even yellowish. It always remains shortest on the head, becoming hair-like and matted elsewhere before the post-juvenal moult. The change of coat is well illustrated by a series of our specimens. The down on the flippers is the first to go; it is then lost from the belly, next from the back, and lastly from the upper breast, throat, and head. Fragments of it cling longest on the neck. For the most part the whole envelopment comes off in the form of tangled mats. For a few days the sprouting contour plumage fails thoroughly to cover the skin of the head and gular region, which is hidden only gradually by the succeeding growth of black feathers. The new plumage of the upper breast reveals a pale yellowish tinge. The auricular patches are yellow, slightly brighter than the breast but without a suggestion of orange. The subtle, greenish yellow gloss or bloom makes its appearance on the crown of the head soon after the down has entirely disappeared. The young King Penguin is then a less glorified replica of its parents, with a weaker, blackish bill. About the time that the juvenals take to sea, toward the end of their second summer, the black lateral plates of the mandibular rami are moulted, the newly exposed surfaces of the shields being white.

Study Questions

ORGANIZATION AND CONTENT

1. Murphy's *Oceanic Birds of South America*, from which these paragraphs are taken, is a large and thorough scientific work containing great amounts of data concerning many different kinds of birds. The type of observation on which scientific description is based is well illustrated by these four paragraphs on young King Penguins. To what extent has Murphy used exact details?
2. Explain what principle of order Murphy followed in arranging the four paragraphs.
3. Which sentences give information regarding size?
4. Which sentences describe the movements of the birds?

5. Are there any details besides those relating to size and movement?
6. Why does the author use figurative language in paragraph 3?

1. What proportion of sentences begin with the subject?
2. What proportion begin with some subordinate element?
3. How many of Murphy's sentences are compound?
4. How do the structure and length of Murphy's sentences compare with those of Kipling's sentences in the preceding selection?

1. Look up *drab, natal, juvenal, regurgitate, oakum, gular, auricular, lateral.*
2. Which of these words are derived from the Latin?
3. List the color adjectives. Which of them show the greatest attempt to be exact?

Imitate Murphy's scientific description by describing some creature through stages of development—a puppy, a kitten, a chicken, a duckling, or even a baby; or take some wild bird or animal that you have observed long enough and with enough concentration to know exactly how it looks and behaves. Or go to the zoo and describe some creature there. Employ details in the same manner that Murphy does.

SHIP-NOISES
by C. S. Forester

There were ship-noises all round him as he ate. Every time the *Lydia* rolled and pitched a trifle as she reached the crest of the swell which was lifting her, the woodwork all creaked gently in unison. Overhead came the sound of Gerard's shod feet as he paced the quarterdeck, and sometimes the pattering of horny bare feet as some member of the crew trotted by. From forward came a monotonous steady clanking as the pumps were put to the daily task of pumping out the ship's bilge. But these noises were all transient and interrupted; there was one sound which went on all the time so steadily that the ear grew accustomed to it and only noticed it when the attention was specially directed to it—the sound of the breeze in the innumerable ropes of the rigging. It was just the faintest singing, a harmony of a thousand high-pitched tones and overtones, but it would be heard in every part of the ship, transmitted from the chains through the timbers along with the slow, periodic creaking.

Study Questions

ORGANIZATION AND CONTENT

1. Description, we have said, has to do with the effects of things on our human senses—on sight, smell, hearing, taste, touch. In this paragraph the author concentrates upon the sounds that a character hears—the captain of a ship as he sits in his cabin eating his dinner. Indicate how the author has made us aware of the directions from which the sounds come.
2. Does this paragraph have a topic sentence?
3. What contrast is brought out in sentence 5?

SENTENCE STRUCTURE

1. Point out the subordinate clauses in sentences 2, 3, and 4.
2. To what extent do sentences 5–6 differ in pattern from 2–4?
3. Has the author given variety to the structure of his sentences, or do they seem monotonous in structure?

DICTION

1. Look up *bilge, transient, overtones, periodic.*
2. There are words that are formed to imitate sounds—such as *hiss, moo, bang.* Forming words of this sort is called onomatopoeia. Are there any such onomatopoeic words in this paragraph?
3. Which words most precisely convey the quality of the "ship-noises"?

ASSIGNMENT

Select a place where one would hear a number of varied sounds and also one steady sound in the background, like the sound of the breeze in the ship's rigging. Some other possibilities include a large railroad station or airport, the driver's compartment of a truck, a laundry, a newspaper office, a manufacturing plant. In your paragraph be sure to select exact words to represent the noises that you describe.

A SCHOOLHOUSE
by Vern Wagner

1 My first glimpse of the White Star School in its weed-grown and treeless yard facing north on the south side of a shallow basin is an indelible memory. The building was alone on the prairie, a little gray, white-trimmed, peaked-roof schoolhouse with two windows on the east and two on the west, fronted by an enclosed entry with a shed roof. A white star was painted on the gable of the building; a short flagpole was fastened above that to the ridgepole. Back of this were two other buildings, an open shed for children to tie their horses in if they rode to school, and the coal house with the boys' toilet on one end and the girls' on the other. In the yard was the pump.

2 The inside of the schoolhouse was calcimined a pale blue with a whitish ceiling. The floor was a worn gray. Desks and seats were scattered about, the kind that are usually screwed to the floor, with iron grill work on the sides and legs. There was a small teacher's desk, an old round coal stove in the middle of the floor with a pipe going up then back to the chimney at the south end, a water cooler on a stand, a large wooden cupboard where books and supplies were kept, a glove hanging from one corner of the ceiling on a pulley, a map case. There was a blackboard across the front of the room, a kerosene lamp in a bracket on the wall, no blinds at the windows, a picture of Lincoln and another of Washington on the back wall. A dusty American flag was fastened above the blackboard. There was also the flagpole outside, a prow on the front gable. There was a windup phonograph with six records, an organ rendition of "Always," the "William Tell Overture," a record to teach the identification

Vern Wagner, "The White Star School," *Western Humanities Review*, Vol. 11 (Autumn, 1957).

of various instruments, and three lesser numbers. The school smelled of stale, locked-in air, as distinctive an odor as that of a beer parlor.

[3]   The school and its yard were haunted with echoes from a quarter century's children, their pulses and shapeless dreams. It was worn, tragic, a country school on the first day following a summer's glad forgetfulness by its young. It had been patient and deserted then but for rare derisive forays made by passing youngsters all through the heat of June, July and August. The building stood there. It did not sit. It stood as the wooden weapon against ignorance and defeat, the house of community hope and of the future. It stood alone on the high upland prairie, braving cold and heat, a land ship on a motionless voyage of discovery into human possibility. It was wholly inspiring. Only in separated views was it depressing. At nineteen, scared as I was, I felt how, above all, upright it was. I was at last a teacher housed in my own school.

Study Questions

ORGANIZATION AND CONTENT

1. What three things about the schoolhouse does the author take up in his three paragraphs?
2. Paragraph 1 lists many details. Which of these details best convey an impression of the school facilities and location?
3. Paragraph 2 also gives many specific details. What feeling do they give you about the schoolhouse?
4. Which of the details are purely informational? Which have something to do with color, shape, or condition?
5. Besides information and sense impressions, what feelings does the author succeed in conveying about the school in paragraph 3?
6. What interpretation does the author give of what the building represented?

SENTENCE STRUCTURE

1. By what means has the author made some sentences especially long—for example, sentences 2 and 4 of paragraph 1, sentences 4 and 5 of paragraph 2?

2. What similarity of pattern do these four sentences have?
3. Point out the shortest sentences in the paragraphs.
4. Do these very short sentences have any special purpose or effect?

DICTION

1. Look up *indelible, derisive, forays.*
2. Are the adjectives more important for their denotative or for their connotative value?
3. Do the adjectives appeal to any other senses than sight?
4. Which are more important in this description, the verbs or the adjectives? Why?
5. Is there a difference in the vocabulary of paragraph 3 and that of paragraph 2?

ASSIGNMENT

Write three paragraphs on a building—the first paragraph on the exterior, the second on the interior, and the third on the feelings that the building created in an observer. Take a church, a country store, a barracks, a camp, a bank, or a hotel. It might be best to select as the subject either a rather new building or an extremely old one. Be sure to note a great many specific details.

A STAGECOACH TRIP
by Charles Dickens

1   The coachman mounts to the box, Mr. Weller jumps up behind, the Pickwickians pull their coats round their legs and their shawls over their noses, the helpers pull the horse-cloths off, the coachman shouts out a cheery "All right," and away they go.

2   They have rumbled through the streets, and jolted over the stones, and at length reach the wide and open country. The wheels skim over the hard and frosty ground: and the horses, bursting into a canter at a smart crack of the whip, step along the road as if the load behind them: coach, passengers, cod-fish, oyster barrels, and all: were but a feather at their heels. They have descended a gentle slope, and enter upon a level, as compact and

Charles Dickens, *The Pickwick Papers* (1836–1837).

dry as a solid block of marble, two miles long. Another crack of the whip, and on they speed, at a smart gallop: the horses tossing their heads and rattling the harness, as if in exhilaration at the rapidity of the motion: while the coachman, holding whip and reins in one hand, takes off his hat with the other, and resting it on his knees, pulls out his handkerchief, and wipes his forehead: partly because he has a habit of doing it, and partly because it's as well to show the passengers how cool he is, and what an easy thing it is to drive four-in-hand, when you have had as much practice as he has. Having done this very leisurely (otherwise the effect would be materially impaired), he replaces his handkerchief, pulls on his hat, adjusts his gloves, squares his elbows, cracks the whip again, and on they speed, more merrily than before.

³   A few small houses, scattered on either side of the road, betoken the entrance to some town or village. The lively notes of the guard's key-bugle vibrate in the clear cold air, and wake up the old gentleman inside, who, carefully letting down the window-sash half-way, and standing sentry over the air, takes a short peep out, and then carefully pulling it up again, informs the other inside that they're going to change directly; on which the other inside wakes himself up, and determines to postpone his next nap until after the stoppage. Again the bugle sounds lustily forth, and rouses the cottager's wife and children, who peep out at the house-door, and watch round the blazing fire, and throw on another log of wood against father comes home; while father himself, a full mile off, has just exchanged a friendly nod with the coachman, and turned round to take a good long stare at the vehicle as it whirls away.

⁴   And now the bugle plays a lively air as the coach rattles through the ill-paved streets of a country-town; and the coachman, undoing the buckle which keeps his ribands together, prepares to throw them off the moment he stops. Mr. Pickwick emerges from his coat collar, and looks about him with great curiosity; perceiving which, the coachman informs Mr. Pickwick of the name of the town, and tells him it was market-day yesterday, both of which pieces of information Mr. Pickwick retails to his fellow-passengers; whereupon they emerge from their coat collars too, and look about them also. Mr. Winkle, who sits at the extreme edge, with one leg dangling in the air, is nearly

precipitated into the street, as the coach twists round the sharp corner by the cheesemonger's shop, and turns into the market-place; and before Mr. Snodgrass, who sits next to him, has recovered from his alarm, they pull up at the inn yard, where the fresh horses, with cloths on, are already waiting. The coachman throws down the reins and gets down himself, and the other outside passengers drop down also: except those who have no great confidence in their ability to get up again: and they remain where they are, and stamp their feet against the coach to warm them—looking, with longing eyes and red noses, at the bright fire in the inn bar, and the sprigs of holly with red berries which ornament the window.

Study Questions

ORGANIZATION AND CONTENT

1. In this selection Dickens tells of one of the famous trips by stagecoach that Mr. Pickwick and his companions made to Dingley Dell. Perhaps the emphasis is more on narrative (story) than on description proper. But how much do we *see* and *hear* while the coach is journeying through one of its stages?
2. *Story* implies a series of events. How does the author make us aware of the passage of time?
3. Try to identify the elements in the writing that make the reader feel action, movement, and adventure.
4. Paragraph 1 consists of a single sentence. Why is it so short?
5. What topic is paragraph 2 mainly about? Paragraph 3? Paragraph 4?
6. How does Dickens distribute the attention which he gives to the coachman, the passengers outside, the passengers inside, the horses, the surroundings?
7. Where does Dickens introduce little touches of humor? Is he laughing at the people of whom he writes?

SENTENCE STRUCTURE

1. Sentence 1 has six clauses. What type of sentence is it, simple, compound, or complex?
2. What is the effect of sentence 1?
3. Does the selection contain any other sentences of the same type?

4. The selection contains a number of *and*'s. Count them. What effect does Dickens achieve by using them?
5. Compare this effect with that of the Kipling selection, which also has numerous *and*'s.

DICTION

1. Look up *exhilaration, precipitated.*
2. Most of the words in this selection are short. Was Dickens right in using so many short words?
3. Why are the verbs especially significant? Which verbs are the most emphatic?
4. Which adjectives and nouns do the most to create a vivid effect?
5. Compare the vocabulary here with that of the previous selections by Dickens.

ASSIGNMENT

Write four paragraphs telling of a journey in a modern vehicle —a bus, a train, or a ship. In a brief first paragraph show the start, in paragraph 4 the arrival, and in paragraphs 2 and 3 something of the journey in between. Imitate Dickens by emphasizing action and movement.

ARRIVAL AT NEW YORK
by John Dos Passos

1   Three gulls wheel above the broken boxes, orangerinds, spoiled cabbage heads that heave between the splintered plank walls, the green waves spume under the round bow as the ferry, skidding on the tide, crashes, gulps the broken water, slides, settles slowly into the slip. Handwinches whirl with jingle of chains. Gates fold upwards, feet step out across the crack, men and women press through the manuresmelling wooden funnel of the ferryhouse, crushed and jostling like apples fed down a chute into a press.

2   On the ferry there was an old man playing the violin. He had a monkey's face puckered up in one corner and kept time

From *Manhattan Transfer*, by John Dos Passos. Copyright by John Dos Passos, published by the Houghton Mifflin Co., 1925.

with the toe of a cracked patent-leather shoe. Bud Korpenning sat on the rail watching him, his back to the river. The breeze made the hair stir round the tight line of his cap and dried the sweat on his temples. His feet were blistered, he was leadentired, but when the ferry moved out of the slip, bucking the little slapping scalloped waves of the river he felt something warm and tingling shoot suddenly through all his veins. "Say, friend, how fur is it into the city from where this ferry lands?" he asked a young man in a straw hat wearing a blue and white striped necktie who stood beside him.

3   The young man's glance moved up from Bud's road-swelled shoes to the red wrist that stuck out from the frayed sleeves of his coat, past the skinny turkey's throat and slid up cockily into the intent eyes under the brokenvisored cap.

4   "That depends where you want to get to."

5   "How do I get to Broadway? . . . I want to get to the center of things."

6   "Walk east a block and turn down Broadway and you'll find the center of things if you walk far enough."

7   "Thank you sir. I'll do that."

8   The violinist was going through the crowd with his hat held out, the wind ruffling the wisps of gray hair on his shabby bald head. Bud found the face tilted up at him, the crushed eyes like two black pins looking into his. "Nothin," he said gruffly and turned away to look at the expanse of river bright as knifeblades. The plank walls of the slip closed in, cracked as the ferry lurched against them; there was rattling of chains, and Bud was pushed forward among the crowd through the ferryhouse. He walked between two coal wagons and out over a dusty expanse of street toward yellow street-cars. A trembling took hold of his knees. He thrust his hands deep in his pockets.

Study Questions

ORGANIZATION AND CONTENT

This is the opening of a novel of 1925. In his description of the ferry slip and of Bud Korpenning's experiences on the ferry as he comes for the first time to New York, John Dos Passos has done his best to turn himself into a camera and record what went on. Dos Passos is noted for his vivid communication of sharp sense impressions.

1. In paragraph 1 you are made aware of what *things?*
2. Of what colors, sounds, and smells do you become conscious?
3. What colors and sounds in the final paragraph?
4. What little details in paragraph 2 show the author's sharp, intense observation? What details in paragraph 3?
5. What function does paragraph 3—a one-sentence paragraph—have?
6. How many similes does the author use? Point them out.
7. Without using similes, are there other ways of saying what the similes say?
8. This selection contains some conversation. Does it sound natural? If so, why? If not, why not?

SENTENCE STRUCTURE

1. In sentence 1 pick out the verbs. What difference would there be if the author had used an *and* before *settles?*
2. Is there any reason why sentence 2 is a short one, between the two longer sentences of paragraph 1?
3. What is the effect of the three clauses in sentence 3?
4. In what other sentences does the author use a pattern of three parallel elements?
5. Note the participial constructions in the first two sentences of the last paragraph. Explain how their effect is different from that of a clause, either main or subordinate.
6. Does the author use more active verbs or passive verbs in his sentences?

DICTION

1. Make a list of the verbs that are used most precisely.
2. Make a list of the most fresh, exact adjectives.
3. Do any of the nouns play as significant a part in the description as do verbs and adjectives?
4. Do you approve of such word combinations as *orangerinds, manuresmelling,* and others of the same kind?

ASSIGNMENT

Describe the arrival of a person at a town or some other place, and show how he made inquiries of someone he met; that is, include some conversation. Give sharp impressions of both the new scene and the people encountered. Or describe how someone came to a football game, a boxing match, or a circus. Or tell how a person arrived at a large office building, made inquiries, and rode in a crowded elevator. Stress not only visual details, but also smells and the textures of things.

A MAN OBSERVING A WOMAN
by *William Sansom*

1   One moment the window was empty, a dark square—and the next this strange new woman was standing against the sill.

2   Her appearance was as sudden as if a blind had been snapped up.

3   There she stood exactly in the centre of her little theatre of sashes and sill and darkness beyond. One expected her to bow.

4   He backed away from his own window like a thief.

5   In between them a wild spring wind drove through the trough of back-gardens, raising sudden birds of white paper, waving the trees, whipping a storm of movement between all the rows of quiet shut windows. But that was outside. In, it was still.

6   He stood back in the room alone and breathless, still slightly crouched, not daring to move about. So quiet alone among the furniture! Sounds from outside echoed in loud to accuse his secret second—a lumber cart rumbling to its cockney cry, a blackbird's sudden pipe, the thrash of a beaten mat. His heart beat loud as a clock, faster than the mat. He thought: Not until that cart has called three times more, I won't move till then—when a blackbird pounded down with a taffeta swish on the window-box, raised its long tail and slowly lowered it in a long breath of arrival, then cocked its head to stare straight in at him.

7   He blushed. He had begun blushing before. Now the pricking flooded pink round his ears: and staring back into the bird's worm-crazy glare he saw how absurd this was and did what he had all this long second been impelled to do—stepped quietly forward again towards the window; but making, though that woman was a full thirty yards away across the short gardens, carefully no sound. The blackbird looked amazed, gave a gulp

and flew off. He started—the little wings thrashed loud like a silk fan—and, with his body carefully turned away from the window opposite, he picked up a book. He opened it, and thus appeared to be reading as now slowly he swivelled round and let his brow-sheltered eyes reach up off the print, keeping his head carefully lowered.

Study Questions

ORGANIZATION AND CONTENT

1. These paragraphs are the opening of an English novel of 1956. The chief character looked out of the window of his apartment and was surprised at the sudden appearance of the woman mentioned in paragraph 1. What feelings and reactions are expressed in the first four extremely short paragraphs?
2. If the author had put the material of the first four paragraphs into one paragraph, what difference in effect would be noticed?
3. Narration and description are combined. Does the selection impress you as mainly narrative or mainly descriptive?
4. There is a stronger psychological element in this selection than in previous ones. Where does the author communicate the psychological reactions of the observer?
5. How would you describe his psychological state?
6. What contrast between indoors and outdoors is made? Why does the author make it?

SENTENCE STRUCTURE

1. Comment on the structure of the three sentences of paragraph 5.
2. What is the function of sentence 2 in paragraph 6?
3. Note how interruptive some of the sentences are: sentence 5 in paragraph 6, sentences 3 and 5 in paragraph 7. Do these interruptive sentences bring the reader closer to the strange experience the man is having—make it easier to follow—or keep him further off, on the outside of it?
4. How does the structure of sentences 1, 2, and 3 of paragraph 7 reflect the content of those sentences?

DICTION

1. Point out which verbs are vivid and emphatic.
2. Does the passage contain any vivid or unusual adjectives?

3. The author makes use of figurative language. Explain how these metaphors function: "theatre" in paragraph 3, "birds" in paragraph 5, "taffeta swish" in paragraph 6, "pricking flooded pink" and "eyes reach up" in paragraph 7.
4. Indicate three similes in the passage. Do they function in the same way as the similes of the selection by Dos Passos?

ASSIGNMENT

Imitate the selection rather closely. Imagine someone (yourself, if you like) looking out of a window and seeing something that surprises, or shocks, or excites him very much. Use one-sentence paragraphs at first. Make a contrast of some kind between indoors and outdoors. Have vivid verbs and metaphorical language. This assignment will allow you to use a good deal of imagination. Try to write with high imaginative voltage.

BATTLE-SCENE
by Audie Murphy

1   A sergeant in the first platoon senses the predicament. If his men are isolated, they will likely be destroyed. He makes his decision quickly. Motioning his men to follow, he rises and with a submachine gun charges head-on toward one of the enemy positions two hundred yards away.

2   On the flat, coverless terrain, his body is a perfect target. A blast of automatic fire knocks him down. He springs to his feet with a bleeding shoulder and continues his charge. The guns rattle. Again he goes down.

3   Fascinated, we watch as he gets up for the third time and dashes straight into the enemy fire. The Germans throw everything they have at him. He falls to the earth; and when he again pulls himself to his feet, we see that his right arm is shattered. But wedging his gun in his left arm-pit, he continues firing and staggers forward. Ten horrified Germans throw down their guns and yell, "*Kamerad.*"

Audie Murphy, *To Hell and Back* (New York, Holt, Rinehart and Winston, Inc., 1949).

Study Questions

ORGANIZATION AND CONTENT

1. This selection is from a famous story of World War II first published in 1949. Certainly it is primarily narrative. Does it contain any parts that might be called descriptive?
2. The three paragraphs are short. Are such short paragraphs suitable in this instance?
3. The three paragraphs are arranged in the order of climax. Explain what each paragraph tells of and why paragraph 3 is the climactic paragraph.
4. The charging sergeant is attacking enemy forces. How does the author represent the two forces in the conflict?

SENTENCE STRUCTURE

1. The sentences are prevailingly short. Are the short sentences suitable?
2. How many of the sentences are simple sentences?
3. How many of them begin with the subject? How many have some modifier before the subject?
4. Do the sentences follow one another smoothly, or is their effect rather choppy?

DICTION

1. In a story of action one might expect verbs to be very important. Are the verbs strong and effective? Which verbs are most effective? Which least effective?
2. How high a percentage of adjectives does the author use? Compare the percentage of adjectives with that of the three preceding selections.

ASSIGNMENT

Write three short paragraphs arranged in the order of climax about some tense moment of action. This might have to do with an incident of military training, an athletic event, a hunting, fishing, or swimming experience, an automobile accident, or an emergency like a storm, fire, or flood. Check your verbs to make certain that they are effective. In each paragraph underline the sentence that you consider to be the most forceful.

II Exposition

Oₙₑ ᴏꜰ ᴛʜᴇ
most important and most often used types of writing is explanation. People are constantly being requested or urged to explain something or other. Explain what was done; explain what it was like; explain how it operates; explain the sequence of happenings; explain what it means; explain how it developed; explain how you felt; explain your position; explain what you think; explain yourself!—these demands for explanations crowd upon all, day after day. These same demands account for the frequency of use and the vast importance of explanatory writing—which, in discussions of composition, is more commonly called exposition.

Though it may certainly deal with things which may be observed by means of the senses, exposition appeals more, however, to the mind than to the senses. Understanding, achieved by the mind, rather than the immediate experience conveyed by the senses, is the chief goal of the expository writer. It is not so much the look or smell or feel of things that the reader gains from exposition as an idea of how they originated, how they developed, how they are organized, how numerous or how complicated they are, how they are related to other things, how significant they are, or what they mean. Description has to do with concrete phenomena and concrete experiences; exposition very often goes beyond the concrete into the region of abstractions, the realm of ideas.

Providing instruction and meeting the needs of the human race for knowledge and understanding—these are the purposes of exposition. Everything found in encyclopedias, handbooks, and dictionaries is exposition. An infantry manual, a manual on constructing family fallout shelters, a handbook explaining the basic movements of square dancing, a pamphlet on methods of insect control—all are examples of exposition; as are likewise such works as a textbook of surgery or a grammar of the French language. Expository writing concerns itself with practical matters; all the reports that provide information for executives, congressmen, mayors, deans, military officers, school superintendents, diplomats, stock analysts, and prime ministers—all these systematic accumulations of data that help in getting the world's work done are pieces of expository writing. Therefore, it may be stated that exposition is practical writing. But, though exposition deals with every practical matter in the world, it is not limited to practical affairs in the workaday sense of the term. The writer of exposition may present ideas on the most theoretical matters too. Books on physics or philosophy, on metaphysics or evolution, highly theoretical, are exposition; but, of course, they are written to satisfy men's practical demands for understanding in all these areas.

Whatever may be the subject of exposition, the writing itself must be systematic and well organized. The simplest type of exposition is an enumeration, a very common and useful way of developing expository paragraphs. Many explanations simply comprise a list of details (with or without actual numbers) to show what something is like or how something is done.

More complex methods of exposition are analysis and definition, which involve classification and division. Whether one is explaining the operation of an airplane or of a frog, he will have to do some analyzing, that is, tell what the parts are and how they are related for purposes of functioning. Likewise, if a student is defining a frog, he must first classify it: obviously it does not belong in the class of vegetables or any nonanimal group. After he has properly classified it, he must then show how it is different from other members of the same class; he must explain what points of difference separate frogs from toads and salamanders.

In all expository writing it is advisable to use examples, analogies, comparisons and contrasts, particularly when the subject is an abstract one. The reader will be able to understand an unfamiliar subject better if it is somehow related to a thing with which he is already familiar. The concept of relativity, for example, can be approached by way of two trains moving at different speeds. Understanding is helped too by systematic comparisons and contrasts: two different groups may be compared or contrasted, two different periods, or men, or theories, or methods of agriculture, or government, or medical treatment. The reader is very likely to learn, to be enlightened, by reading a thoughtful comparison. A comparison or contrast, based on various points of resemblance or difference, will have been made possible by an act of analysis.

All of these matters will become clearer as the apprentice writer studies the examples given in the various sections of the text. Though some of the selections in the section on description have contained a small amount of exposition, the readings in the present section contain very little that is not expository.

ENUMERATION

The writer of exposition must understand his material thoroughly enough to be able to organize it clearly according to some scheme which the reader can follow and understand. It has been noted that the simplest type of exposition is enumeration: a certain number of things exist or are our concern. These are the things, or the parts, or the steps: one, two, three, four. Much the same is the arrangement of items in chronological order, one, two, three, four, from the earliest to the latest. When we are dealing with a systematic arrangement of things in space rather than in time, we can take them up according to a spatial order: one, two, three, four from right to left or from left to right, from top to bottom or from bottom to top. Such an arrangement may seem rather arbitrary, but it has the great virtue of clarity. A reader will hardly get lost during the explanation.

✳ ✳ ✳

A LUNCH IN LEBANON
by Ralph and Molly Izzard

Observing the size and bulk of our hosts, we had reasoned that they kept a good table. We were not disappointed. Mme. Kanaan, flushed and perspiring in her pink silk *peignoir*, had been busy in her kitchen ever since our arrival, and through the bathroom walls we had caught many shrill chidings and upbraidings and a clattering of pots from the kitchen next door. We lunched alone in a vast deserted dining-room, sparsely furnished with an elaborate sideboard and a chandelier. The spotless tablecloth was covered with a multitude of *hors d'oeuvres*, the characteristic *Meze* of the Levant. This alone was the equivalent of an entire coffee-shop lunch. Next came a favourite dish: a great platter of snowy rice, accompanied by another platter of French beans in a gravy of braised tomatoes and titbits of tender lamb. A smiling maid encouraged us all to have second helpings, and, this done, we were then presented with a steak each, chips and a large bowl of salad. A certain glaze began to appear over the eyes of the party and the two men had recourse to the small bottles of *arak* to stimulate their appetite. A rice pudding next appeared, sweetened with rosewater, as a treat for the children, Elias rashly having informed our hostess that the children were very fond of this Arab sweet. Then came water-melons, grapes and enormous apples, and hot, sweet cups of coffee, and at last we were done.

Study Questions

ORGANIZATION AND CONTENT

1. How much description is in this paragraph? How much narration? How much exposition?

From *A Walk in the Mountains* by Ralph and Molly Izzard. Copyright © 1959, by Ralph and Molly Izzard. Courtesy of David McKay Company, Inc.

2. How much of the paragraph is concerned with people? How much with the place where the lunch was served?
3. How many main items of lunch are listed?
4. How many other things are itemized?
5. Instead of first, second, third, and so on, what terms do the authors use to indicate the separate items?
6. What problem of organization did the authors solve? How did they know what to place first in the paragraph? Last?

SENTENCE STRUCTURE

1. Participial phrases appear in sentences 1, 3, and 4. Is there any reason why each of them should be in a different position in the sentence?
2. How much variation is there in the length of the sentences?
3. How much variety of sentence structure is there?
4. Does the paragraph contain an excessive number of *and*'s connecting parts of sentences?

DICTION

1. Which words give an impression of the dining-room?
2. Which words give an impression of people?
3. Look up *peignoir, hors d'oeuvres, arak (arrack)*. Why are they italicized in the text?
4. Look up *chidings, upbraidings, Levant, braised, titbits*.
5. Is there any difference between *size* and *bulk*?

ASSIGNMENT

Write one solid paragraph about a meal, enumerating the different courses or servings of food. Give the reader some impression of the place where the meal was served and of the people who prepared and/or served it. The material will probably not be interesting unless you write about a meal that is extraordinary; it may seem interesting because of its length, richness, or strangeness. You might write about a family picnic, a Christmas dinner, or some special feast, perhaps one with unusual foreign dishes.

THE UNITED STATES CAPITOL

by Allen Drury

"This building," one of the Capitol guides was telling the day's first batch of tourists, listening attentively in the great rotunda, "stands on Capitol Hill 88 feet above the level of the Potomac River, on a site once occupied by a subtribe of the Algonquin Indians known as the Powhatans, whose council house was located at the foot of the hill. The building covers an area of 153,112 square feet, or approximately 3½ acres; its width, including approaches, is 350 feet. It has a floor area of 14 acres, and 435 rooms are devoted to offices, committees, and storage. There are 679 windows and 554 doorways. The cornerstone of the Capitol was laid on Sept. 18, 1793. The northern wing was completed in 1800, and in that small building the legislative and judicial branches of the government, as well as the courts of the District of Columbia, were housed in that year when the government moved here from Philadelphia. The southern section of the Capitol was finished in 1811, the House of Representatives then occupying what is now known as Statuary Hall. At that time a wooden passageway connected the two wings. This was the situation when the Capitol was burned by the British on August 24, 1814, entering up the narrow, winding steps known as the British Stairway which you will see later in your tour."

Study Questions

ORGANIZATION AND CONTENT

1. Which parts of this paragraph would you call description? Narration? Exposition?
2. What things are itemized in the first four sentences?
3. What idea governs the order in which sentences 5–9 are arranged?
4. Do sentences 5–9 also contain itemizing?
5. What elements of sentences 5–9 cause them to differ in content from sentences 1–4? Does the difference cause the paragraph to lack unity?

6. Contrast the purpose and the effect of this paragraph with the purpose and effect of the one on "A Lunch in Lebanon" and the one on "Fox How" by Mrs. Ward.

SENTENCE STRUCTURE

1. What does the parenthetical material about the guide and the tourists accomplish in sentence 1?
2. Is there any advantage in placing this material where it is? Would it be more effective if placed in a different position?
3. Sentence 1, rather long, is a "loose" sentence; the thought is completed early, and the sentence continues with a string of modifiers. Is the sentence too long? Does it seem unlikely that any one would speak so long a sentence?
4. The sentences of the paragraph are linked together by constant references to what?
5. Why should sentences 2–5 be as short as they are?

DICTION

1. The vocabulary is not difficult. Look up the roots of: *rotunda, legislative, judicial.*

ASSIGNMENT

Write a paragraph in which you give similar information about a building—a public building in your town, a university building (perhaps the oldest building on the campus), or some other one about which you gather material. Some of it you can obtain by your own observation.

THE WAY OF LIFE OF CITIZENS OF A SMALL CITY *by Plato (Benjamin Jowett, trans.)*

Let us then consider, first of all, what will be their way of life, now that we have thus established them. Will they not produce corn, and wine, and clothes, and shoes, and build houses for themselves? And when they are housed, they will work, in summer, commonly stripped and barefoot, but in winter substantially

Plato, *The Republic,* translated by Benjamin Jowett (1871).

clothed and shod. They will feed on barley-meal and flour of wheat, baking and kneading them, making noble cakes and loaves; these they will serve up on a mat of reeds or on clean leaves, themselves reclining the while upon beds strewn with yew or myrtle. And they and their children will feast, drinking of the wine which they have made, wearing garlands on their heads, and hymning the praises of the gods, in happy converse with one another. And they will take care that their families do not exceed their means; having an eye to poverty or war.

Study Questions

ORGANIZATION AND CONTENT

1. In *The Republic* of Plato Socrates discusses with friends the founding of a community. It is founded on the principle of division of labor, of mutual help. Then Socrates explains how the citizens will live. What is the key idea of the topic sentence of the paragraph?
2. What are the functions of sentences 1 and 2?
3. In what way does the last sentence differ from the other sentences?
4. Why should it be the concluding sentence instead of being placed elsewhere in the paragraph?
5. Food, shelter, and clothing are the main items that the citizens will first need. What more detailed information does the paragraph give regarding each item?

SENTENCE STRUCTURE

1. What words appear in every sentence of the paragraph that link the sentences together?
2. Show how participial phrases are used in sentences 4, 5, and 6.
3. Indicate parallelism of structure among the participial phrases.
4. In which sentences does some kind of parallelism appear?

DICTION

1. Look up *corn* (it is used here according to European usage, not American). What word would an American translator probably have used instead of *corn?*
2. Why should the beds be strewn with yew or myrtle?
3. Which words suggest that the citizens' way of life is a good one?

The paragraph is about an easily imagined community that doubtless resembles a small wholesome city of ancient Greece. In a city like New York or a small town in the Scottish Highlands or the Great Plains or a coal-mining region the details would be different. Write a paragraph explaining the way of life of some actual (not imagined) community that you know. Set down details that are somewhat less general than those of the model.

QUALITIES OF THE AMERICAN BUSINESS MAN *by Harold Laski*

The American business man has certain remarkable qualities in an exceptional degree. His vitality is extraordinary. He lives his business from morning to night; he gives to it the devotion that a medieval saint gave to his religion. He is almost always experimental about it, eager to take a chance, anxious to change from one vocation to another if the latter seems to offer additional opportunities. He believes profoundly in the possibilities of machinery; and he is almost always willing to take the long rather than the short view. He knows, as no other people but the Germans and, since 1917, the Russians know, the value of *expertise* and research. He assumes that success in a business calling is of itself a title to influence, and since there are few men who do not desire influence, he agrees with but little difficulty that the successful business man ought to be respected. There is, indeed, an important sense in which it is true to say that for most Americans the acquisition of wealth is a form of religious exercise; that is why, perhaps, a well-known advertiser could write, in the twenties, of Jesus Christ as a successful business man without the public feeling that there was some incongruity in the thesis.

Study Questions

ORGANIZATION AND CONTENT

1. What expectation does the first sentence arouse in the reader?
2. What is the key word in the first sentence?
3. If you were to number the items that the author presents for proof of his main idea, how many numbers would you have to use?
4. Which statements explain what the businessman does? What he believes? What judgments he makes about the importance of business?
5. Is the last sentence properly placed? If you think so, explain why it should appear last and not earlier.
6. Why might the author think that the idea of Jesus Christ as a successful businessman is incongruous?

SENTENCE STRUCTURE

1. How are the sentences linked together?
2. What words provide the links?
3. Most of the sentences begin in the same way. What advantage has the author gained by beginning them thus?
4. The last two sentences are the longest, each divided into two parts. Explain how each part is organized.

DICTION

1. Look up *vitality, medieval, profoundly, expertise, incongruity, thesis.*
2. How many adjectives has Laski used in his discussion? How vivid are the adjectives?
3. Are adjectives, nouns, or verbs the most significant words of the paragraph?

ASSIGNMENT

Write a similar paragraph listing the qualities of someone who is not a businessman: a farmer, a lawyer, a civil service worker, a truck driver, a professor, a grammar school teacher, or some other representative of an occupation. Include as many qualities as Laski does in the model paragraph.

THACKERAY'S EXPERIENCE IN AMERICA *by Lionel Stevenson*

He found himself enjoying America much more than he had expected. The unaffected friendliness and interest made him feel at home, and he confessed in a letter to Kate Perry that "the jolly manner answers here very well, which I have from Nature or Art possibly." He admired the ladies, who struck him as being "as lean as greyhounds" and "all dressed like the most stunning French actresses." He loved the "rush and Restlessness," the fast-moving traffic on Broadway, the railway trains puffing into the very heart of the city, the houses being pulled down to make way for new ones, the barricades and scaffoldings in every street. All the residences he visited seemed to be in the process of remodeling, with carpenters hammering and the stairs or a wall torn out. The furnishings were like those of "the most splendid gambling houses ... The houses are all so new that the walls are not even papered, and on the walls in the midst of the hangings of brocade and the enormous gold frames and mirrors you see little twopenny pictures and coloured prints." He summed up New York as being "the most curious varnish of Civilization."

Study Questions

ORGANIZATION AND CONTENT

1. The English novelist William Makepeace Thackeray visited the United States as a lecturer in 1852. This paragraph from a biography of Thackeray explains one phase of his visit. What is it? What words express the topic idea?
2. How many different details are listed to prove that this idea is true?
3. Some of the evidence presented in the paragraph is in the form of quotations from Thackeray's letters. (This is a good illustration of the way in which such quotations may be introduced into paragraphs.) Which of the quotations is most effective?
4. Why did the author choose the last quotation to place in the final sentence?

Lionel Stevenson, *The Showman of Vanity Fair*. Copyright 1947, by Charles Scribner's Sons.

1. To what extent does the author vary the length and the organization of his sentences?
2. Which sentences are the shortest? The longest?
3. Do any simple sentences appear in the paragraph?
4. What words does the author repeat in order to link the sentences together and provide transition?

DICTION

1. Look up any words that you do not know.
2. Which words present the most *specific* details?
3. Which words most strongly suggest qualities of New York life?

ASSIGNMENT

Read an account of some other visitor to a foreign land (a biography, an autobiography, or letters), and find out whether he liked it or not. Then explain in one paragraph what things made him like or dislike the country. Introduce four or five quotations from statements or letters of the visitor that will support the topic theme.

DR. ARNOLD'S URGE TO EXPRESS HIS IDEAS *by Arthur Penrhyn Stanley*

It was of course only or chiefly through his writings, that he could hope to act on the country at large; and they accordingly, almost all, became inseparably bound up with the course of public events. They were not, in fact, so much words as deeds; not so much the result of an intention to instruct, as of an incontrollable desire to give vent to the thoughts that were struggling within him. "I have a testimony to deliver," was the motive which dictated almost all of them. "I must write or die," was an expression which he used more than once in times of great public interest, and which was hardly too strong to describe what he felt.

Arthur Penrhyn Stanley, *Life and Correspondence of Thomas Arnold* (1844).

If he was editing Thucydides, it was with the thought that he was engaged, "not on an idle inquiry about remote ages and forgotten institutions, but a living picture of things present, fitted not so much for the curiosity of the scholar, as for the instruction of the statesman and the citizen." (Pref. vol. iii, p. xxii.) If he felt himself called upon to write the History of Rome, one chief reason was, because it "could be understood by none so well as by those who have grown up under the laws, who have been engaged in the parties, who are themselves citizens of our kingly commonwealth of England." (Pref. vol. i, p. vii.) If he was anxious to set on foot a Commentary of the Scriptures, it was mostly at times, when he was struck by the reluctance or incapacity of the men of his own generation to apply to their own social state the warnings of the Apostles and Prophets. If he was desirous of maintaining against the Oxford school his own views of the Church, it was that, "when he looked at the social condition of his countrymen," he "could not doubt that here was the work for the Church of Christ to do, that none else could do it, and that with the blessing of her Almighty Head she could." (Serm. vol. iv. Pref. p. cxv.)

Study Questions

ORGANIZATION AND CONTENT

1. This paragraph tells us that Dr. Thomas Arnold, famous nineteenth-century schoolmaster and scholar, had a strong urge to express his ideas. On what topics and for what purpose did he particularly desire to express them?
2. In order to illustrate, and to prove, his assertion about Dr. Arnold, the author lists several pieces of evidence. Number them in order.
3. Is this evidence strong and convincing, or not?
4. If so, what makes it strong; if not, what makes it unconvincing?

SENTENCE STRUCTURE

1. The paragraph contains eight sentences. In what way do sentences 5-8 differ from sentences 1-4?
2. The use of parallel grammatical structure often helps the reader to see that ideas are equal in weight and function and thus helps him to understand a paragraph rapidly. Point out how the

author has used parallel grammatical structure in some of his sentences.

3. Explain how certain ideas of this paragraph are equal in weight. Equal in function.
4. Why does the author introduce quotations into the paragraph? What is their source?
5. The paragraph was written in the nineteenth century. Some of the punctuation is different from what is usual in the twentieth century. In what places would a twentieth-century writer be likely to use punctuation different from that of Stanley?

DICTION

1. Look up *reluctance, incapacity, Apostles, Prophets.*
2. Stanley alludes to Thucydides. Identify him and the work he wrote.
3. The "Oxford school" is identified with Tractarianism. What view of the Church of England did it represent?
4. Is Stanley's vocabulary mainly general or particular, concrete or abstract? Too much so?

ASSIGNMENT

Gather information about a noted scientist, artist, architect, writer, physician, educator, or public leader. Write a paragraph to illustrate that the person believed strongly in some idea or principle. In your paragraph present several pieces of evidence to prove your point. Include some quotations among the evidence. Use parallel grammatical structure in the same way that Stanley does.

REASONS FOR NEGATIVE INFLUENCE OF ISLAM IN AFRICA *by George W. Carpenter*

1   What does the Islamization of an African people mean in terms of its capacity to utilize the resources of Western culture and to continue in the stream of development to which contact

George C. Carpenter, "The Role of Christianity and Islam in Contemporary Africa," in C. Grove Haines, ed., *Africa Today* (Baltimore, The Johns Hopkins Press, 1955).

ANALYSIS

Another method of exposition, somewhat different from the mere listing of details, is called analysis. One may wish to set down a record of something, that is, to make a list: for example, these are the tools of a miner, these are the generous acts of Herod, these are the typical activities of Catherine II. On the other hand, one may wish to explain what conclusions he has reached by thinking about some subject in an analytical way. The process of analysis is a process of taking something apart— not ripping it apart and throwing the parts about helter-skelter but taking it apart in a thoughtful, systematic manner so that one can see the parts clearly and understand how they are related to each other. It is rather like "factoring" a problem. Analysis is one of the chief ways by which the human mind deals with the world. The mind can seldom understand anything immediately as a whole; it cannot "take in" an undivided subject very conveniently. It does not feel satisfied that it has properly done its work of thinking unless it knows that it has divided whatever *can* be divided or has classified whatever *can* be classified.

So the writer, when he explains something by the method of analysis, "thinks out" his subject; he divides a thing into parts, or he arranges items according to some scheme of classification. It would be difficult to explain the construction or the operation of an airplane, for example, without mentioning the different parts of the airplane. Merely listing all the parts (as if one were making up a catalogue of supplies) will not help a reader to understand the construction or operation of an airplane. A writer will have to cut up the airplane, as it were—that is, show what chief functioning areas an airplane designer must take into consideration: the power plant, the fuselage, the guiding apparatus, the landing gear, the instruments. Then, of course, he can subdivide and explain what the parts of each main area are and how they relate to each other. Thus, we may see that analysis, as a form of expository writing, goes beyond enumeration although it also makes some use of enumeration.

The process of analysis as it might be applied to the topic of *an airplane* has just been illustrated. But suppose the topic is *airplanes.* In this case the writer will take his subject apart in a different fashion—by means of classification. He will tell about air-planes according to types: such as heavy, medium, and light; or fighters, bombers, passenger planes, and cargo planes; or pro-peller-driven planes, turboprop planes, and jet-propelled planes. When one is classifying, the important rule that he must follow is to use principles that are logically parallel for his "files" or "bins" of classification. There would be an illogical hodgepodge if it were stated, "Airplanes fall into the following classification: jet-propelled, passenger, and medium." The three principles of method of propulsion, function, and weight would be mixed up. Such illogical classifying would not help the reader; it would only confuse him. Classification, then, must be made according to logical principles.

Both of these methods of explanation, analysis by partition and analysis by classification, are very commonly used. When one is discussing topics such as those mentioned above or explaining, for example, how something is made, he will use analysis. If one has to explain how steel is produced or how paper is made, he will analyze the process of production, that is, divide it into its parts and explain each step. It is readily evident how enormous is the field of exposition by analysis. It is, therefore, extremely impor-tant that the apprentice writer train himself to be efficient in this type of writing.

※ ※ ※

TYPES OF AZTEC SETTLEMENT
by G. C. Vaillant

According to the environment, be it forested or semi-arid and consequently open, there tend to be two types of settlement. In dry, open country the minerals which plants need remain near the surface, so that fields can be farmed over and over again. The people, therefore, can maintain a permanent village. Forest country, on the other hand, presents a serious problem to Stone Age people. To clear ground for planting, trees must be girdled and, after they die, burned. The soil therefore rapidly becomes exhausted and incapable of supporting crops. The Indians met this situation in two ways: by moving the entire village, or by allowing each family group sufficient land so that crop rotation would permit exhausted fields to recover by lying fallow. This last method tended to decentralize the population except in very small communities.

Study Questions

ORGANIZATION AND CONTENT

1. According to what division does the anthropologist G. C. Vaillant discuss types of Aztec settlement?
2. Call the first item of the division A and the second, B. Which one is further subdivided, A or B? Identify the subdivisions.
3. Identify the topic sentence of the paragraph.
4. What has the author really explained in this paragraph?
5. What is the function of the last sentence in the explanation?

SENTENCE STRUCTURE

1. What term has the author repeated in sentence 2 so as to link it to sentence 1?

2. What word in sentence 3 provides transition from sentence 2 to sentence 3?
3. What phrase in sentence 4 gives a signal for a change in thought?
4. Point out parallel phrasing for parallel ideas in sentence 7.

DICTION

1. Vaillant's language is quite easy; but look up the roots of the following words: *environment, arid, consequently, permanent, rotation, fallow.*
2. From what languages do these roots originally come?

ASSIGNMENT

Write one paragraph of about 150 words in which you develop the idea that there are different types of communities that you know of; or different types of houses in a community; or different types of people who live there; or different types of "comic" strips or of automobiles. In your paragraph indicate what chief causes have produced the differences between the types. Underline transitional words and phrases in your paragraph.

PAINTING

by Leon Battista Alberti

Painting is divided into three parts, a division we have taken from nature. Since painting tries to represent seen things, let us observe in what way objects are seen. In the first place, when we see an object we say it is a thing that occupies a place. The painter describing this space will call this marking of the edge with a line *circumscription* or outline. Then, looking it over, we observe that many surfaces in the seen object connect, and here the artist, setting them down in their proper places, will say that he is making the *composition*. Lastly, we determine more clearly the colors and the qualities of the surfaces. Since every difference in representing these arises from light, we may call it precisely the *reception of light* or illumination. Thus painting is composed

From Elizabeth Holt, *A Documentary History of Painting* (Princeton, N.J., Princeton University Press, 1957).

of *circumscription, composition,* and the *reception of light.* In the following, each will be discussed briefly.

Study Questions

ORGANIZATION AND CONTENT

1. What is the topic sentence of this paragraph?
2. The three parts into which Alberti divides the process of painting are related by means of what?
3. How has the author emphasized the key terms of his explanation?
4. What is the function of the next-to-last sentence? Of the last sentence?

SENTENCE STRUCTURE

1. What words are used as signals to provide transition in the paragraph?
2. Sentence 2 and two other sentences begin with dependent clauses. Explain what advantage there is in beginning these sentences with dependent clauses.
3. *Painting* is the subject of two main clauses. Is there any advantage in choosing other terms as the subjects of all the other clauses?

DICTION

1. Look up the roots of *circumscription, composition, reception, illumination.*
2. From what language are these words borrowed?
3. Give other words using the same roots.

ASSIGNMENT

Write a paragraph explaining your analysis of some kind of work, a paragraph that might serve as an introduction to a more detailed discussion of the subject. You might write on studying, showing the essential activities that a person must perform in order to study effectively. Or, in the same way as Alberti, write a paragraph indicating the basic operations involved in preparing a meal, making a garden, planting a tree, having a successful meeting.

ERECTING STEEL STRUCTURES
by Joseph Mitchell

In the erection of steel structures, whether bridge or build-ing, there are three main divisions of workers—raising gangs, fitting-up gangs, and riveting gangs. The steel comes to a job already cut and built up into various kinds of columns and beams and girders; the columns are the perpendicular pieces and the beams and girders are the horizontal ones. Each piece has two or more groups of holes bored through it to receive bolts and rivets, and each piece has a code mark chalked or painted on it, indicating where it should go in the structure. Using a crane or a derrick, the men in the raising gang hoist the pieces up and set them in position and join them by running bolts through a few of the holes in them; these bolts are temporary. Then the men in the fitting-up gang come along; they are divided into plumbers and bolters. The plumbers tighten up the pieces with guy wires and turnbuckles and make sure that they are in plumb. The bolters put in some more temporary bolts. Then the riveting gangs come along; one raising gang and one fitting-up gang will keep several riveting gangs busy. There are four men in a rivet-ing gang—a heater, a sticker-in, a bucker-up, and a riveter. The heater lays some wooden planks across a couple of beams, mak-ing a platform for the portable, coal-burning forge in which he heats the rivets. The three other men hang a plank scaffold by ropes from the steel on which they are going to work. There are usually six two-by-ten planks in a scaffold, three on each side of the steel, affording just room enough to work; one false step and it's goodbye Charlie. The three men climb down with their tools and take their positions on the scaffold; most often the sticker-in and the bucker-up stand on one side and the riveter stands or kneels on the other. The heater, on his platform, picks a red-hot rivet off the coals in his forge with tongs and tosses it to the sticker-in, who catches it in a metal can. At this stage, the rivet is shaped like a mushroom; it has a buttonhead and a stem. Mean-while, the bucker-up has unscrewed and pulled out one of the

Joseph Mitchell, *The Mohawks in High Steel* (New York, Farrar, Straus and Cudahy, Inc.). Copyright © 1959, by Joseph Mitchell. Reprinted by permission of Harold Ober Associates, Inc.

temporary bolts joining two pieces of steel, leaving the hole empty. The sticker-in picks the rivet out of his can with tongs and sticks it in the hole and pushes it in until the buttonhead is flush with the steel on his side and the stem protrudes from the other side, the riveter's side. The sticker-in steps out of the way. The bucker-up fits a tool called a dolly bar over the buttonhead and holds it there, bracing the rivet. Then the riveter presses the cupped head of his pneumatic hammer against the protruding stem end of the rivet, which is still red-hot and malleable, and turns on the power and forms a buttonhead on it. This operation is repeated until every hole that can be got at from the scaffold is riveted up. Then the scaffold is moved. The heater's platform stays in one place until all the work within a rivet-tossing radius of thirty to forty feet is completed. The men on the scaffold know each other's jobs and are interchangeable; the riveter's job is bone-shaking and nerve-racking, and every so often one of the others swaps with him for a while. In the days before pneumatic hammers, the riveter used two tools, a cupped die and an iron maul; he placed the die over the stem end of the red-hot rivet and beat on it with the maul until he squashed the stem end into a buttonhead.

Study Questions

ORGANIZATION AND CONTENT

1. In this piece of exposition analysis is applied to the workers, the material, and the process. Explain how the workers and the material are divided into parts.
2. Why does the author have to speak about the workers and the material before he explains the process?
3. The author does not number the steps in the process. How does he make clear the passing from one step to another?
4. How are the classes of workers fitted into the sequence of operations? Which class receives the most attention?
5. Make an outline indicating the divisions and subdivisions of the workers.
6. What is the purpose of the last three sentences?

SENTENCE STRUCTURE

1. Is this a substantial paragraph? How many sentences does it contain?
2. How long are the sentences—shortest? Longest? Average length?
3. How many of the sentences begin with the subject instead of with a subordinate element?
4. How many sentences have a straightforward subject-verb-complement construction?
5. Is the sentence construction suitable for the topic which is being explained?
6. What grammatical constructions has the author used for introducing the divisions and subdivisions of things analyzed?

DICTION

1. Make a list of the active verbs used in this paragraph. How many sentences contain such verbs?
2. What is the difference between a *crane* and a *derrick?* What are the sources of these words?
3. Explain the relationships among *maul, malleable,* and *mallet.*
4. Explain what gives *pneumatic, pneumatology,* and *pneumonia* a common element.
5. How can words so different as *scaffold* and *catafalque* have a common origin?
6. Is the author's style either too formal or too informal? Does he use chiefly a formal or a colloquial vocabulary?

ASSIGNMENT

Analyze a process and explain the steps required. Some suggestions are:

1. The operation of an office, indicating what workers are needed and their duties
2. The production of a newspaper
3. The construction or the operation of a chicken house
4. The organizing of an efficiently managed picnic or other outing for a considerable group of people
5. Spraying fruit
6. Preparing a flower bed, from the first step to the blooming of the flowers
7. Making a pond
8. Raising dogs, pigs, or cattle from birth to maturity

HOUSING SITES
by Sir Francis Bacon

Houses are built to live in, and not to look on: Therefore let use be preferred before uniformity; except where both may be had. Leave the goodly fabricks of houses, for beauty only, to the enchanted palaces of the poets: Who build them with small cost. He that builds a fair house, upon an ill seat, committeth himself to prison. Neither do I reckon it an ill seat, only, where the air is unwholesome; but likewise where the air is unequall; as you shall see many fine seats, set upon a knap of ground, environed with higher hills round about it: whereby the heat of the sun is pent in, and the wind gathereth as in troughs; so as you shall have, and that suddenly, as great diversity of heat and cold, as if you dwelt in several places. Neither is it ill air only, that maketh an ill seat, but ill ways, ill markets; and, if you will consult with Momus, ill neighbors. I speak not of many more: want of water, want of wood, shade, and shelter; want of fruitfulness, and mixture of grounds of several natures; want of prospect; want of level grounds; want of places, at some near distance, for sports of hunting, hawking, and races; too near the sea, too remote; having the commodity of navigable rivers, or the discommodity of their overflowing; too far off from great cities, which may hinder business; or too near them, which lurcheth all provisions, and maketh every thing dear: where a man hath a great living laid together, and where he is scanted; all which, as it is impossible, perhaps, to find together, so it is good to know them, and think of them, that a man may take as many as he can: and if he have several dwellings, that he sort them so, that what he wanteth in the one, he may find in the other.

Study Questions

ORGANIZATION AND CONTENT

1. This paragraph is taken from Sir Francis Bacon's essay *Of Building*, which was published in 1625. No doubt Bacon had

Sir Francis Bacon, *Bacon's Essays and Colours of Good and Evil* (London, 1883).

observed many English houses before he wrote this paragraph. What mental classifications was he making during his observations?
2. By his discussion of housing sites and their shortcomings, what is Bacon trying to show the reader?
3. Explain what the metaphor in sentence 3 contributes to the discussion.
4. To what extent does Bacon make use of enumeration in this analytical paragraph?

SENTENCE STRUCTURE

1. This paragraph represents the language, punctuation, and sentence style of the early seventeenth century. Point out the places where a modern writer would be likely to use different punctuation marks from Bacon's.
2. How has Bacon used the principles of balance and contrast in the sentences of this paragraph?
3. Indicate the function of the conjunctions *and, or, but* in this respect.
4. Why does Bacon use so much repetition in sentences 5 and 6?

DICTION

1. Bacon's seventeenth-century vocabulary will require you to look up some of his words; note that nearly all of these words are still in use but have changed their meanings or are not usual in American usage. Look up *uniformity, fabricks, unequal, environed, several, ways, fruitfulness, prospect, commodity, lurch, sort, want.*
2. Some of Bacon's words seem to have been chosen for alliteration or other sound values. Point out examples in sentences 1–4.
3. Bacon mentions Momus. This is a literary allusion. In one of Aesop's fables Momus was asked to judge a house built by Athena. He complained that it should have had wheels so that it could be moved away from bad neighbors.

ASSIGNMENT

Imitate this paragraph, using *books, horses, dogs, clothing, a used car, a college education, or a life work* as the opening term. Analyze the subject in terms of its desirable and undesirable qualities or in terms of a right and a wrong attitude toward it. Use balanced sentence elements, as Bacon does, to illustrate both sides.

ROBINSON CRUSOE'S DWELLING
by Daniel Defoe

1   My thoughts were now wholly employed about securing myself against either savages, if any should appear, or wild beasts, if any were in the island; and I had many thoughts of the method how to do this and what kind of dwelling to make, whether I should make me a cave in the earth or a tent upon the earth. And, in short, I resolved upon both, the manner and description of which it may not be improper to give an account of.

2   I consulted several things in my situation, which I found would be proper for me: first, health and fresh water; secondly, shelter from the heat of the sun; thirdly, security from ravenous creatures, whether men or beasts; fourthly, a view to the sea, that if God sent any ship in sight, I might not lose any advantage for my deliverance, of which I was not willing to banish all my expectation yet.

3   In search of a place proper for this I found a little plain on the side of a rising hill, whose front towards this little plain was steep as a house-side so that nothing could come down upon me from the top; on the side of this rock there was a hollow place worn a little way in like the entrance or door of a cave, but there was not really any cave, or way into the rock at all.

4   On the flat of the green, just before this hollow place, I resolved to pitch my tent. This plain was not above a hundred yards broad and about twice as long, and lay like a green before my door and at the end of it descended irregularly every way down into the low grounds by the seaside. It was on the north-northwest side of the hill, so that I was sheltered from the heat every day, till it came to a west and by south sun, or thereabouts, which in those countries is near the setting.

5   Before I set up my tent, I drew a half circle before the hollow place, which took in about ten yards in its semi-diameter from the rock and twenty yards in its diameter, from its beginning and ending.

6   In this half circle I pitched two rows of strong stakes, driving them into the ground till they stood very firm like piles, the biggest end being out of the ground about five foot and a half and

Daniel Defoe, *The Life and Strange Surprizing Adventures of Robinson Crusoe, of York, Mariner* (1719).

sharpened on the top. The two rows did not stand above six inches from one another.

⁷ Then I took the pieces of cable which I had cut in the ship, and laid them in rows one upon another, within the circle, between these two rows of stakes, up to the top, placing other stakes in the inside, leaning against them, about two foot and a half high, like a spur to a post; and this fence was so strong that neither man nor beast could get into it or over it. This cost me a great deal of time and labor, especially to cut the piles in the woods, bring them to the place, and drive them into the earth.

⁸ The entrance into this place I made to be not by a door, but by a short ladder to go over the top, which ladder, when I was in, I lifted over after me, and so I was completely fenced in, and fortified, as I thought, from all the world, and consequently slept secure in the night, which otherwise I could not have done.

Study Questions

ORGANIZATION AND CONTENT

1. Defoe's famous character Robinson Crusoe explains in eight short paragraphs the constructing of his dwelling on his island. What does he accomplish in paragraph 1? In paragraph 2?
2. After reading paragraph 2, what would you expect in the rest of the explanation?
3. This piece of exposition has some likeness to the two preceding examples. How does it resemble the paragraph by Bacon? The one by Mitchell?
4. The paragraphing here might be called journalistic; that is, several of Defoe's paragraphs are extremely short, like those in a modern newspaper. Which paragraphs consist of only one sentence each?
5. Explain which of Defoe's paragraphs might logically be combined into longer paragraphs.
6. What topic sentences would you have to invent for new, longer paragraphs?
7. Where, in this selection, are you aware of the act of analysis?

SENTENCE STRUCTURE

1. How has Defoe used balanced phrasing and balanced grammatical constructions in sentence 1?

2. Where does grammatical balance appear in paragraph 2?
3. Which are the three longest of Defoe's sentences? Does their length make them hard to understand? Explain why it does or does not.
4. Defoe's *Robinson Crusoe* was published in 1719, nearly a century later than Bacon's *Essays*. Does his use of the colon and semicolon resemble Bacon's, or not?

DICTION

1. Defoe's language is quite simple. Are there any words that you need to look up?
2. Does Defoe use simpler, commoner, less technical words than Bacon?
3. List the conjunctions that Defoe uses. Which ones does he use most?
4. What is the effect, in terms of sentence length and complexity, of these conjunctions?

ASSIGNMENT

Write three or four paragraphs explaining why some place in which you have lived was very pleasant or very unpleasant. You will have to analyze such things as its situation, arrangement, and particular facilities. Or, if you have ever built a camp, explain, after the manner of Robinson Crusoe, how you did it. Or write three or four paragraphs that tell what your plan would be for an ideal home. Underline the topic sentences of your paragraphs.

ARISTOCRACIES by *Thomas Jefferson*
(*from a letter to John Adams, 1813*)

I agree with you that there is a natural aristocracy among men. The grounds of this are virtue and talents. Formerly, bodily powers gave place among the *aristoi*. But since the invention of gunpowder has armed the weak as well as the strong with missile death, bodily strength like beauty, good humor, politeness, and other accomplishments has become but an auxiliary ground of distinction. There is also an artificial aristocracy, formed on wealth and birth, without either virtue or talents; for with these

From *The Writings of Thomas Jefferson,* The Thomas Jefferson Memorial Association (Washington, 1903).

it would belong to the first class. The natural aristocracy I consider as the most precious gift of nature for the instruction, the trusts, and government of society. And, indeed, it would have been inconsistent in creation to have formed man for the social state and not to have provided virtue and wisdom enough to manage the concerns of society. May we not even say that that form of government is the best which provides the most effectually for a pure selection of these natural *aristoi* into the offices of government. The artificial aristocracy is a mischievous ingredient in government, and provision should be made to prevent its ascendancy. On the question what is the best provision, you and I differ, but we differ as rational friends, using the free exercise of our own reason and mutually indulging its errors. You think it best to put the pseudo-*aristoi* into a separate chamber of legislation, where they may be hindered from doing mischief by their co-ordinate branches and where, also, they may be a protection to wealth against the agrarian and plundering enterprises of the majority of the people. I think that to give them power in order to prevent them from doing mischief is arming them for it and increasing instead of remedying the evil.

Study Questions

ORGANIZATION AND CONTENT

1. Jefferson has divided aristocrats into what main kinds?
2. What are the bases of each category?
3. Set down Jefferson's pattern of division, using Roman numerals and capital letters.
4. What do sentences 2 and 3 contribute to the discussion?
5. At what point does Jefferson begin to discuss the functions of aristocrats in government?
6. Explain in your own words why he differed with John Adams on this point.

SENTENCE STRUCTURE

1. What methods of transition has Jefferson used in his sentences —repetition of important words, pronouns, special transitional terms?
2. In how many of the sentences do the key terms of the discussion appear?

3. Has Jefferson placed these key terms in his sentences so as to give them emphasis?
4. What contrast is indicated by the phrasing of the last two sentences?

DICTION

1. Look up *aristocracy*, aristoi, *auxiliary*, *pseudo*, *agrarian*.
2. From what languages have these words been taken?

ASSIGNMENT

Write a paragraph like Jefferson's in which you analyze:

1. Your college class in terms of its qualities or its backgrounds
2. Student organizations in terms of the students' experience or environment
3. Teachers in terms of their classroom behavior
4. Classes in terms of their attitudes toward learning

AN ANALYSIS OF AMERICAN SOCIETY
by David Riesman

1   . . . One way of looking at American society at present is to divide it into two groups of people: one, a relatively small white-collar and professional group who work long hours and bear disproportionate responsibilities; and the other, a relatively large group who work short hours (even if one does not include coffee breaks) and bear few taxing responsibilities. This latter group includes the millions of forty-hour-per-week workers, of thirty-hour-per-week school children, and of retired people.

2   American life is, of course, unevenly mechanized and systematized, and the first-named group must fill in for America's deficiencies—and rise to its challenges—out of their personal energies and at the frequent expense of their own budget of leisure and ease. Some in this group of people are industrial managers, well-paid in money and prestige for worrying about productivity, the meaning of which has been extended to include employee morale, health, psychological security, and general happiness; and for

David Riesman, "Thoughts on Teachers and Schools," *The Anchor Review*, Vol. I (New York, Doubleday & Co., Inc., 1955).

worrying about selling a product, a transaction which now embraces many novel private and public services (budgeted for under "good will"). Some in this group of people are high civil servants, paid neither in money nor in unambiguous prestige for worrying about the resentments of the rest of the world. Some of these people are doctors, paid with very great prestige and moderately great fees for working sixty- and seventy-hour weeks to repair the health of a nation which can increasingly afford health, and which redefines it to extend from the somatic to the psychosomatic to the psychosocial, and from the cure of acute illness to the prevention of debility and the extension and beatitude of the life span. And some of the people in this first group of overtime worriers are professors, perhaps increasingly bitter about pay and prestige, and more harassed in trying to make sense of their data (too much of it, and too equivocal), of each other (more conferences, committees, and projects than ever), and of their students (more of whom can now afford college and fewer of whom, for reasons we shall examine, come with elementary literacy). Even so, these professors' pay and prestige, if it appears low to them, is worlds above that of most public school teachers, and the latter also have many more compulsory classroom hours (though there are a few, in the best city and suburban systems, who will fare better financially than, for instance, a classics professor at a small non-ivy campus). Indeed many members of this first group are "paid" for their long hours by the variety and freedom their work permits: they prefer accepting even wearisome responsibilities to enduring meaningless routines under others' supervision.

3   Public school teachers are, in all probability, the largest aggregation of those who, themselves left behind by industrial advance and the general shortening and lightening of hours, must supply much of the energy for that advance and much of the training for the work-free future of their pupils. Teachers are in fact the archetype of these white-collar functionaries, who, in helping bring about a society of greater abundance, have their own official and unofficial lives torn and complicated in the process. The teaching function, since it does involve the training or "guidance" of children for an era of abundance, has been extended to include training in group co-operation, manners, the arts, and self-understanding, as well as in large residues of the traditional curriculum. Teachers, therefore, are under growing

pressure to provide a "happy and rounded atmosphere" in the classroom, while they themselves lead lives of harried desperation, not only because of the multiplying demands of the classroom, but because of the many "voluntary" activities expected of them: advising the dramatics or journalism club, consulting with parents, participating in civic and church groups. Many feel they must use their "vacations" attending summer school to acquire needed credits, or earning extra money with summer camps.

Study Questions

ORGANIZATION AND CONTENT

1. What preliminary division of American society does Riesman perform in paragraph 1?
2. What act of subdivision is performed in paragraph 2?
3. Show the division and subdivisions by making an outline of paragraphs 1 and 2.
4. How is paragraph 3 related to paragraph 2?
5. What are the bases of the division made in paragraph 1?
6. In what terms is "pay" represented in paragraph 2? Are these terms used consistently with each subgroup?
7. Does the author mean in paragraph 2, sentence 1, that American life should be "evenly mechanized and systematized"? If it were, what changes would be required?
8. Look up *irony* and *paradox*. Then explain what is ironical or paradoxical in paragraph 3.

SENTENCE STRUCTURE

1. Explain the functions of the three parts of sentence 1: the part before the colon, the one between the colon and the semicolon, and the one after the semicolon.
2. What is the grammatical relation of *workers, children,* and *people* in sentence 2?
3. What repetitions does the author use to provide good transitions in all three paragraphs?
4. Parallel grammatical constructions represent an important element of sentence style in paragraph 2. Show exactly where and how they are used.
5. The second half of paragraph 2 has four parentheses, the first three in one sentence. Do these parentheses clog the sentence, or do they perform a significant function?

1. Look up *prestige, novel* (adj.), *unambiguous, somatic, psycho-somatic, debility, beatitude, equivocal, literacy, aggregation, archetype, functionaries, residues.*
2. The roots of all these words are important. Learn their meanings. From what languages do they come?
3. Explain the difference between *morale* (paragraph 2) and *moral.*
4. What is the meaning of "disproportionate responsibilities" in paragraph 1?
5. The author has placed quotation marks around a number of words: "good will" and "paid" in paragraph 2; "guidance," "happy and rounded atmosphere," "voluntary" and "vacations" in paragraph 3. Why?
6. David Riesman is a famous sociologist; is his vocabulary highly technical? Is it difficult?

ASSIGNMENT

Write an analysis of a group similar to Riesman's: you might divide a college student-body on the basis of curricular efforts and extracurricular activities, and the honors or "pay" that go with them; or citizens of any community on the basis of civic activities. Or you might make a division of stores, dogs, sports, or types of clothing in terms of function or prestige.

TYPES OF CORAL REEFS
by F. D. Ommanney

1   There are three main types of coral reef. The first is the fringing reef which lies just off the main shore, separated from it by a narrow and shallow lagoon. It is this kind of reef which encircles Mauritius like a girdle, leaving between itself and the coast of the island a shallow stretch of water, in places only a few hundred yards wide but in others, as at Grand Port, expanding to a width of two miles or more. Fringing reefs, too, encircle many of the islands that we visited such as Coëtivy and Agalega and, though irregular and broken in places, lie off parts of the

From *The Shoals of Capricorn.* Copyright 1952, by F. D. Ommanney. Reprinted by permission of Harcourt, Brace & World, Inc.

coasts of Mahé and Praslin in the Seychelles. Down the east coast of Africa from Cape Guardafui to the coast of Portuguese East there runs an almost continuous coral reef which is mostly of the fringing type.

2   The second type is the barrier reef, which lies at a much greater distance from the coast than the fringing reef and may be several miles wide with many channels through it, and is separated from the mainland by a wide lagoon. The most famous example of this type is the Great Barrier Reef off the eastern coast of Australia. It is over a thousand miles long. In its northern half the barrier may not be more than 20 or 30 miles from the Queensland coast, but in its southern half it is as much as 50 or 100 miles from the coast and consists of several parallel reefs with channels between them.

3   The third type of reef is the atoll, a ring of growing corals crowned with palm trees, often hundreds of miles from any true land and rising abruptly in the ocean from a depth of thousands of fathoms. In the Chagos Islands we found true atolls at Diego Garcia and Peros Banhos, irregular rings of coral rock and sand on which a lush vegetation has taken root, and on which plantations have long been cultivated by man. In the Aldabra group also, 700 miles south-west of the Seychelles, we found coral reefs of varying degrees of perfection.

Study Questions

ORGANIZATION AND CONTENT

1. What is the purpose of the first sentence in each of the three paragraphs?
2. Explain by what principle Ommanney has classified coral reefs.
3. Besides telling the reader the characteristics of each kind of coral reef, what does Ommanney do in his paragraphs?

SENTENCE STRUCTURE

1. In paragraph 1, sentences 2, 3, and 5 have relative clauses introduced by *which*, and paragraph 2, sentence 1 has a similar clause. Some of these are restrictive clauses. Are they punctuated correctly? Should some of them really be nonrestrictive?
2. How are participial phrases balanced in sentence 3?

3. In sentence 4 *reefs* is the subject of what verbs?
4. Note how *too* is tucked away after *reefs* in sentence 4; in the latter part of the sentence this adverb is balanced by what adverbial element similarly placed?

DICTION

1. Why does Ommanney mention so many far-away place names?
2. Point out terms used for transition in these paragraphs.
3. To what extent has the author used a technical vocabulary?

ASSIGNMENT

Analyze, as Ommanney does, some type of thing with which you are familiar—banks, grocery stores, games, vocations, moving pictures would offer good possibilities. Classify according to a single principle, and give several examples of each type that you mention.

REQUIREMENTS OF A COLLEGE PRESIDENT *by Mary Bell Decker*

1   Now that my husband has served fifteen years as a president —a young "old man" in the game as tenure goes—the question, What is a university president? is still not neatly answered, but certain clear challenges must be accepted.

2   The first of these is educational leadership. The president should serve as a perennial gadfly to the trustees, faculty, students, alumni and community generally, spurring them on toward the ideal institution. He should have formulated an educational philosophy which should be understood and approved before he is appointed. He should then explore, initiate and engineer new ideas, or revitalize old ones, that advance this philosophy. A university involves the exchange of many points of view and the sharing of responsibilities, but exchange and sharing are not enough. Too often they simply reduce the character of the institution to the least common denominator. The president, as leader, must find ways to reach out toward the highest common denominator. The university has a responsibility to protect itself from

Clarence R. Decker and Mary Bell Decker, *A Place of Light* (New York, Hermitage House, Inc., 1954). Reprinted by permission of Clarence R. Decker.

fanatics and fools in its presidency, but the danger in American education is not fanaticism or foolishness, but mediocrity. The wear and tear of administrative life erodes conviction in too many administrators, yet conviction must be encouraged and honored if universities are to be something more than a Madame Tussaud wax works.

3 Happy indeed the chief executive who can catalyze without contention, synthesize without strife. In the pioneering days of William Rainey Harper at Chicago, riots among students and protests from faculty were not infrequent. Woodrow Wilson's efforts to introduce innovations at Princeton—innovations that seem mild today—were fought by the graduate dean and alumni. Alexander Meiklejohn's experiments at Amherst led to his dismissal and the resignation of some twenty sympathizing faculty members. Robert Hutchins' leadership at Chicago provoked continuous controversy. A professor visiting us some years ago from one of the great institutions then installing a new president, when asked about the incoming president, exploded: "I don't know anything about him, but I hope he has the good sense to let the faculty alone!" It was an obvious rebuke to the outgoing president, whose three predecessors, having done just that, had bequeathed him an institution in the doldrums. Granted that he had stirred up excitement over important academic matters—surely a major function of a university—the record is clear that over a period of two decades this university was strengthened in its democratic organization and, at the same time, transformed into one of the most provocative and productive in the world.

4 A second obligation of the president is custodianship. He should guard jealously both the freedom and responsibility essential to effective teaching, research and public service. The vast knowledge universities possess today was acquired in no small part from the independent, nonconformist thought of the past— the former heresies that became current orthodoxies. The university must protect itself from within and from without—within, from incompetence, mediocre conformity and fanatical partisanship; without, from "isms" and other special interests of the extreme right or left or—perhaps more dangerous—of the dead center who find universities convenient whipping boys. In times of tension like the present—when teachers' oaths, Congressional investigations, loyalty tests and a variety of anti-intellectual forces

intimidate the profession—the task of protecting the untrammeled search for truth cannot be taken lightly.

⁵ A third obligation of the president is administration. Many look upon administration with disdain, but, like good housekeeping, it is at least a necessary evil and can spell the difference between a wasteful and a useful academic organization. Perhaps more than any other type of corporation, a university, in the old phrase of Pasquier, is "built of men." It is the living spirit of the many individuals who, in one way or another, vitalize its primary function as a center of thoughtful life. The president directs and coordinates the numerous agencies that compose the complex structure of the university; integrates the complete program; seeks the best personnel available; informs the faculty and trustees of the work, needs and opportunities of the institution; and makes recommendations that look toward constant improvement. Through his personal leadership, custodianship, and administration, the distributed and continuous initiative of the various groups and individuals is directed toward the common purpose of the institution.

Study Questions

ORGANIZATION AND CONTENT

1. This selection comprises five paragraphs. What relation does paragraph 1 have to the other four?
2. What are the qualifications of a university president that the author discusses? Where is each one first mentioned?
3. What is the relation of paragraph 3 to paragraph 2?
4. Why does the author refer to Harper, Wilson, Meiklejohn, and Hutchins?
5. What happens in the second half of paragraph 3?
6. What terms are repeated in paragraph 2 to provide transition?
7. How is transition attained in paragraphs 3, 4, and 5?
8. What is the purpose of the last sentence of paragraph 5?

SENTENCE STRUCTURE

1. Several sentences in this selection contain dashes. For what purposes? Are dashes overused?
2. Point out balance and alliteration in paragraph 3, sentence 1. What is the effect of these devices in this sentence?

3. Indicate parallel phrasing in paragraph 4.
4. Which sentences in the selection are the shortest?
5. What special purpose or purposes do the shortest sentences accomplish?
6. Is there enough variety of sentence length in these paragraphs?

DICTION

1. Look up *tenure, perennial, philosophy, initiate, revitalize, fanatics, mediocrity, erodes, catalyze, synthesize, innovations, controversy, doldrums, custodianship, nonconformist, heresies, orthodoxies, partisanship, anti-intellectual, untrammeled, disdain, academic.*
2. From what languages have these words been taken?
3. What does *engineer* (paragraph 2, sentence 3) mean as a verb?
4. Note that the author uses figures of speech (simile, metaphor) to explain what a university president must do. Identify the basic figures of speech used for this purpose.
5. Does the author use too many long words? Too many abstract terms?

ASSIGNMENT

Analyze the qualifications necessary in a person who wishes to win scholastic honors; win athletic honors; be a leader in student organizations; succeed in a particular area of study such as mathematics, literature, science, engineering; or be an effective minister or priest. Write at least one paragraph about each qualification. Compose a final sentence for the same purpose as that of Mrs. Decker.

NEEDS OF UNIVERSITIES
by Margaret Clapp

1   Consider, in general terms, contemporary universities. Learning power, teaching power, research power, purchasing power—those are their needs the world around. And those were their needs in the nineteenth century, with the exception of research power in the earlier part of that century.

Margaret Clapp, "Contemporary Universities: Some Problems and Trends," in Margaret Clapp, ed., *The Modern University* (Ithaca, N.Y., Cornell University Press, 1950).

² Today, the first need among universities everywhere, though it has been less talked about and perhaps less thought about in America than in Europe, is learning power, which is native ability plus the will to learn. An able person, intellectually inquiring, re-flective, and industrious—with learning power, and with leisure in the day after acquiring the necessities for life—can make himself educated, cultured, and wise in this era of free public libraries, museums, and archives. A great teacher can speed the process. But if learning power is not there, the greatest teaching is only of partial value. A student cannot be lifted beyond the limits of his ability.

³ A great teacher may and often does inspire an individual student who heretofore has lacked the will or full opportunity to learn, and so sets the student on the road to education. But if large numbers of students arrive at the university without a solid academic foundation on which to build, the quality of university education must suffer. That problem causes anxiety today, everywhere, though in varying degrees.

⁴ Professors exiled from Germany in the days of Hitler, who have since returned, speak frequently of the thirst for knowledge among German youth. They speak also of the confusion of thinking, the weakness, as compared with former competence, in mathematical and linguistic tools, the large areas of ignorance and distortion resulting from unbalanced textbooks and inadequate libraries, and, added to those offspring of Nazi and war necessity, the effect upon morale of years of physical privation. Students are less well prepared, they say (hastening to qualify with numerous instances a dangerously large generalization).

⁵ Lacking the thorough preparatory work of the old gymnasia, too many German students need a slower pace at the universities than formerly. Nor have they, to the same degree as an earlier generation, the habit of openmindedness in seeking truth, or faith in the value of such a habit. That should be temporary. But given the continued pall of fear and bitterness and given privation that makes the immediately useful all-important, speedy recovery of the universities in Germany is questionable.

⁶ In Great Britain and America, where freedom of thought was never seriously curtailed and where varieties of opinion were easily heard, the problem of the mind stunted by government in-

tent has not existed. But other factors in these countries have led to questions concerning the maintenance of student quality. Temporarily there was the problem of the veteran. The universities looked forward to their arrival with enthusiasm and, it must be admitted, with concern lest the veterans be unable to adapt to university procedures and ideals. Soon after they came, all alarm was dispelled. In its place grew admiration and respect for the remarkable industry and mature effectiveness of the veteran-student whose college or university education had been interrupted when war came.

7   Later, when veterans whose schooling had been broken off at an earlier level reached the universities after intensive, speeded-up preparatory courses, the situation changed somewhat. The ambition and drive were still there, but general information, competence from habit-forming practice in tool subjects and methodology, and experience in intellectual investigation beyond the fixed requirements had, in many instances, suffered from time-saving, semieducational short cuts. That, too, was a temporary problem, to be blamed on the war, not on the students, and was so recognized.

8   But it suggests an aspect of the problem of learning power which remains with us. So far as America is concerned, the issue was evident long before the 1940's, the war and the ensuing dangerous years serving only to speed its rate of growth. It stemmed from a wise insistence, voiced in nineteenth-century Britain as in America, on higher education for the many as a means to national welfare and even national preservation. Arguments used sixty years ago in behalf of widespread high school education in America, and used thirty years ago in behalf of widespread college education in America and of certain courses at such institutions as London University, are now heard relative to sending large numbers of students into most branches of advanced university study: such education is conducive to economic advancement, cultural enrichment, and responsible citizenship.

9   Those are sound arguments. But unless individual students have the ability and the will, in short, unless they have learning power, the ideal for individual and nation cannot be approached. It is not enough for the older generation to offer all young people two decades of schooling, or even sixteen years of it, unless it

makes sure at every stage that students with learning power are neither held back by a slow pace nor unsoundly passed upward, and unless, somehow, young people see in education a right to be cherished, not a burden to be tolerated.

Study Questions

ORGANIZATION AND CONTENT

1. This selection by Margaret Clapp, President of Wellesley College, is an example of analysis on a broader scale than are the previous selections. What are the chief factors that the author points out in analyzing the needs of contemporary universities? How many factors are mentioned?
2. How much space is given to the discussion of the first factor?
3. Which factors are not discussed here? Why not?
4. Why is an element of definition necessary early in paragraph 2?
5. Anxiety is mentioned in the last sentence of paragraph 3. How is this idea followed up in paragraphs 4, 5, and 6?
6. What new aspect of the problem is introduced in paragraph 6?
7. In what way does paragraph 7 contrast with paragraph 6?
8. How are paragraphs 8 and 9 related to the main factor being discussed?
9. What things may bring about weakness of learning power?
10. Should the material of paragraph 9 be put in a separate paragraph?

SENTENCE STRUCTURE

1. How is sentence 2 constructed so as to give emphasis to the key terms?
2. What is the function of the repetition in sentence 3?
3. Both paragraphs 2 and 3 contain a sentence beginning with *but.* What particular purpose do these sentences accomplish?
4. Which sentences in paragraphs 5, 6, and 7 begin with some subordinate element and not directly with the subject?
5. Make shifts in the position of the subordinate elements in these sentences, and decide what advantages there may be in having them where the author has put them.
6. Explain how particular emphasis is placed on the end of sentence 3, paragraph 8.

7. What is the basis of the arrangement of the material in sentence 4, paragraph 8?
8. Which sentence of paragraph 9 has repetition that links it to paragraph 2?

DICTION

1. Look up *contemporary, archives, distortion, generalization, gymnasia, pall, privation, curtail, conducive*.
2. What are the meanings of the roots in *contemporary, archives, distortion, gymnasia, privation, conducive?*
3. From what languages are these words derived?
4. Is the vocabulary of this selection more abstract or more concrete than that of the selections by Decker and Ommanney?

ASSIGNMENT

Analyze the abilities and performance of the best student you know, and explain in three or four paragraphs why he does so well. Be sure to use specific examples to show just how this student arranges and conducts his life. Or treat in the same way the poorest student you know. Or write three or four paragraphs on the best qualities of your own college or university; or on its weaknesses. Or analyze the needs of your home community.

DEFINITION

If someone is asked to "define" a word, he knows that he is expected to explain the meaning of that word, and he may be able to give a satisfactory explanation of the meaning—that is, a definition. On the other hand, he may flounder; his attempt at a definition may be inefficient. There is an efficient way to make a definition, and one should always have it in mind when setting forth meanings of terms.

In the first place, the word *define* has as its root the Latin word *finis*, which means *limit*. If a limit is placed on something, a line is drawn, either physical or mental, beyond which no one can go. To put a limit to a term is to draw a line around it, to mark a line between the meaning of that term and the meanings of all other terms. By doing so, one is saying, "This is the territory which properly belongs to this term; over there beyond the

line is the territory which properly belongs to that other term."
When any word is defined in an efficient way, it is necessary
to take two steps. One must: (1) put the word in the right class;
(2) explain what different qualities the word has from every other
word that also belongs in that class. This is rather like making a
map. The people of the United States are spoken of as Americans;
yet there is a line between New York and Pennsylvania and another line between Pennsylvania and Ohio. The Americans of
New York do not vote, pay taxes, or buy licenses in Pennsylvania,
and though in some communities two Americans live only a block
apart, one will vote for a governor of New York and the other
for a governor of Pennsylvania because there is a map line drawn
between these two men's houses.

If someone asks for a definition of *marble*, one would tell him
first that it is a kind of rock. Thus the first step would be taken;
the term would be put in the right *class*. It has now been established that marble is not a bird or a plant or a liquid; it is a rock.
Of course, there are many other kinds of rocks. How is one to
know marble from granite, for example? He will know by understanding the differences between marble and granite. If the class
called *rock* is compared to the map of the United States, then the
territory within that class called *marble* is like the state territory
called New York, and the territory within that class called *granite*
is like the state territory called Pennsylvania. What the definer
has done is draw mental lines on the class-map between marble
and granite.

Every correct definition has as its basis the two-step operation: placing in class—showing differences.

The class in which a term is placed should not be too large.
If one is asked to define a *cabin* and he states, "A cabin is a thing,"
he has made a poor start. He might also say, "A fork is a thing."
As a class, *thing* is much too general. Somewhere between the
most *particular* term and the most *general* term there will be a
term that will most efficiently classify the word being defined. A
cabin is something like a hut, shack, mansion, or house. All of
these are *dwellings*. *Dwelling* is a more general term than *cabin*.
A dwelling could be classified as a *building*. A building would be
placed in the class of *structures*. A *structure* is "something constructed." Thus, a structure is a *thing*.

So from the most general term to the least general term one goes through the series—thing-structure-building-dwelling-cabin. When defining *cabin*, a more efficient definition will be made if *cabin* is included in the class of *dwelling* rather than in some more general class.

In the same way one might go through another series of gradually narrowing classes, from thing to living thing to animal to mammal to human being to man to hero. If an attempt is being made to define *hero*, it will clearly be better to place the term in the class of *man* rather than in *animal* or even in *mammal*. Thus, having classified a hero as a man, one must show how he is different from all other men. A hero is a man acting in a certain way; the second step is explaining how the ways in which a hero acts are different from the ways of other men.

A word that is a name for a particular object can sometimes be explained most easily by simply pointing to the object—thus if one points at a tree or shovel or table, a quick definition without words is given. Such words stand for concrete things; they are called *concrete* terms. But what if it is necessary to define a term that does not stand for a concrete thing? How can *honesty* or *generosity* be defined? These are *abstract* words, which express a quality or characteristic. It is possible to say, "The man gave back to its owner a purse containing $100." The sentence tells of a concrete action. It would be an example to support such a statement as "He has often shown his honesty." "The owner of the purse showed his generosity by rewarding the man for his honesty." This sentence contains two abstract words, or *abstractions*—words representing qualities, words without a material basis such as *tree* or *shovel* has. But both of these abstractions, *generosity* and *honesty*, can be illustrated. "The owner showed his generosity by giving him a ten-dollar bill." When defining abstractions, one is constantly impelled to illustrate their meanings by using concrete examples. In general, whenever one uses abstract words, he will "come down" from the mental area of ideas (honesty, sweetness, condition) to the physical area of concrete objects and actions. Suppose a storekeeper says, "Economic conditions are bad." Just what does he mean? Furthermore, is he right? What evidence does he have about those abstract "conditions"? Suppose he gives evidence: "Ten of my customers, young married men who work for the steel company, have been laid off." From such concrete evidence his idea at once becomes clearer. The concrete and the specific are of much value in the process of definition.

Very often people know fairly well what the meaning of a word is. However, they have not considered it carefully; they do not know its meaning as well as does an expert or a careful thinker who has taken the trouble to consider it. Therefore, the type of exposition known as definition encountered in books and articles is somewhat more extensive than the definitions found in dictionaries. Such "extended definitions" are likely to be written to answer one or more of the following questions: In precisely what sense is the word being used? Just how much does this term take in? What new sense does the word now include? Regardless of other uses, or the general use, of the word, just what is its basic meaning?

Some writers may write pages or whole chapters that can be called definition. But even though their work is far more extensive than the definitions of a dictionary-maker, these writers will always take the two essential steps of classification and differentiation. Then they may discuss the problem of classification— why one class is better than some other one that people have previously used—or they may discuss differences at length. They may go to some trouble to show what the word does *not* include —what is outside of the limit that should mark the meaning; they may give illustrations and make comparisons that are helpful; they may analyze the term, showing what its different parts are and explaining each part and its relation to the other parts; they may tell the reader something of the history of the word and why certain meanings developed as they did. Whatever methods they use, they are always using their minds to try to communicate a sharper and clearer idea or a broader and more stimulating idea of the meaning of the word.

Both analysis and definition are much used and highly important types of writing. The apprentice writer needs to practice them until he is efficient, for in life today he will never be able to avoid them.

A GENTLEMAN

by James Fenimore Cooper

The word "gentleman" has a positive and limited signification. It means one elevated above the mass of society by his birth, manners, attainments, character and social condition. "Gentleman" is derived from the French *gentilhomme*, which originally signified one of noble birth. This was at a time when the characteristics of the condition were never found beyond a caste. As society advanced, ordinary men attained the qualifications of nobility, without that of birth, and the meaning of the word was extended. It is now possible to be a gentleman without birth, though, even in America, where such distinctions are purely conditional, they who have birth, except in extraordinary instances, are classed with gentlemen. To call a laborer, one who has neither education, manners, accomplishments, tastes, associations, nor any one of the ordinary requisites, a gentleman, is just as absurd as to call one who is thus qualified, a fellow. The word must have some especial significance, or it would be synonymous with man. One may have gentlemanlike feelings, principles and appearance, without possessing the liberal attainments that distinguish the gentleman. Least of all does money alone make a gentleman, though, as it becomes a means of obtaining the other requisites, it is usual to give it a place in the claims of the class. Men may be, and often are, very rich, without having the smallest title to be deemed gentlemen. A man may be a distinguished gentleman and not possess as much money as his own footman.

Study Questions

ORGANIZATION AND CONTENT

1. What misuse or misunderstanding of the word *gentleman* would cause Cooper to write sentence 1?

James Fenimore Cooper, *The American Democrat* (1838).

2. According to sentence 2, in what class does the word *gentleman* belong? What are the differences between a *gentleman* and all other members of the area in which *gentleman* has been classified?

3. How does sentence 3 relate to sentence 2? How does sentence 5 relate to sentence 2?

4. In sentence 5 Cooper says that "society advanced." What sort of "advancement" does he presumably mean?

5. In sentence 5 Cooper says that "the meaning of the word was extended." According to his explanation, why was it extended? What example in sentence 6 provides evidence that the meaning was extended?

6. What is the point of Cooper's mentioning the laborer in sentence 7? What connection does sentence 7 have with sentence 1?

7. In sentences 7, 9, and 10 Cooper shows what a gentleman is *not* (that is, he denies that certain supposed differences between a gentleman and other members of the class really *are* differences). What are the three false differences that Cooper eliminates?

8. Both sentence 11 and sentence 12 are related to sentence 10. Explain what different functions sentence 11 and sentence 12 have in the definition.

SENTENCE STRUCTURE

1. Sentences 3, 4, 5, and 6 indicate differences in time. In which part of the sentences is the time element indicated?

2. Why are the sentences constructed thus?

3. In how many of the sentences does the word *gentleman* or its equivalent appear to provide transition?

4. Explain how sentences 10, 11, and 12 are arranged so as to give strong emphasis to the idea that Cooper is expressing.

DICTION

1. Look up the following words and show from what roots in what languages they were originally derived: *positive, limited signification, caste, synonymous, distinguished.*

2. In what special sense does Cooper use the word *birth*?

3. *Attainments* is a very general term. What specific examples of attainments do you think Cooper might have mentioned if he had gone into more detail?

4. In sentence 9 Cooper mentions *liberal attainments*. He contrasts

these with what other qualifications? Look up *liberal*. Apparently it is an important term. What do you think is the difference between *liberal* attainments and any other attainments?

ASSIGNMENT

1. The term "ladies and gentlemen" is used a good deal in English. Write a one-paragraph definition of *lady* like Cooper's definition of *gentleman*. Obtain some of your information by studying dictionaries. Tell a little about the origin and history of the word. But, having classified the word, use most of your space to show what makes a lady different from all other members of the same class. You may wish, as Cooper did, to rule out some falsely supposed differences.
2. Cooper says in sentence 7 that it would be absurd to call a man who has the qualifications of a gentleman, a *fellow*. After some dictionary study, write a definition of the word *fellow*, following the directions above.

CIVIL ENGINEERING
by Paul J. Brennan

1   Civil Engineering is a profession responsible for providing major physical needs of man. The principal activities of this profession include the planning, design, analysis, and construction of major structures, transportation routes and terminals, water and waste water systems; the use and control of the forces of nature, the control of the environment, and the development of land areas. Public health and natural resources conservation are areas of special import to the civil engineer.

2   Historically, the civil engineer is concerned with such facilities as bridges, buildings, highways, railways, airports, harbors, canals, tunnels, dams, reservoirs, water supply systems, water purification plants, waste water treatment plants, flood control, and many other similarly diverse activities.

3   The planning, design, analysis, research, management, and

Paul J. Brennan, "Liberal Education through Civil Engineering," *Syracuse University Alumni News*, Vol. 42 (Spring, 1961).

construction of these facilities are usually done by the civil engineer as a member of the consulting engineering office, industrial firm, construction firm, governmental agency, research laboratory, university, or private business firm. It is also of interest to note that many civil engineers are integral members of engineering groups that are developing and designing aircraft structures, space vehicle structures, and space navigational methods. They are among those planning facilities for space travel and the habitation of other planets and are active in phases of the use and control of nuclear power.

4   Many of these activities benefit large numbers of people in a community, a region, or an entire nation, and civil engineering activities are thus closely allied with the economics, sociology, law, public administration, political science, climatology, geology, and geography of the environ. Although the civil engineer is not proficient in these disciplines he needs some knowledge of them and limited ability in them in order to evaluate and recognize problems beyond the scope of engineering and to consult with persons who are competent in these areas. This then is the broad field the University graduate in civil engineering enters.

Study Questions

ORGANIZATION AND CONTENT

1. In what class does the author place the term *civil engineering?* What are some other terms that would also be placed in that same class ?
2. What differences does the author point out between *civil engineering* and other terms of the same classification?
3. What is the relation of paragraph 2 to paragraph 1? The relation of paragraph 3 to paragraph 2?
4. What term used in the first sentence of paragraph 3 makes the transition from paragraph 2, and what term in the first sentence of paragraph 4 makes the transition from paragraph 3?
5. In sentence 2 of paragraph 1 there is a list of items, and paragraph 2 consists largely of a list of items. Which items are the more general, which the more specific?
6. What is the function of sentences 2 and 3 of paragraph 3? The function of the last sentence of paragraph 4?
7. Dr. Brennan is the Chairman of the Department of Civil En--

gineering at Syracuse University. This material defining *civil engineering* was published in the Syracuse University *Alumni News* as part of a discussion of the education of the civil engineer, and particularly the civil engineering curriculum in college. Point out how paragraph 4 is related to the topic of engineering education.

SENTENCE STRUCTURE

1. The sentences contain several lists of items. Explain by what grammatical means the different lists are introduced into sentence 2 of paragraph 1, the single sentence of paragraph 2, sentences 1 and 2 of paragraph 3, and sentence 1 of paragraph 4.
2. Why did the author use a semicolon in sentence 2?
3. In which sentences do the words *civil engineering* or *civil engineer* occur? In what grammatical situations do they occur?
4. Does this selection have good sentence variety or not?

DICTION

1. Look up the following words and show from what roots in what languages they were originally derived: *economics, sociology, climatology, geology, geography, proficient, disciplines.*
2. What is the difference between *climate* and *climatology?*
3. Is there a difference between *discipline* and *a discipline?*
4. How is the *environ* (noun) related to *environ* (verb)?

ASSIGNMENT

Just as Brennan explained the work of a civil engineer, and beginning in exactly the same manner as he did, explain what work is done by a nurse, librarian, carpenter, salesman, artist, physician, farmer, teacher, chemist, policeman, minister, electrician, undertaker, or jeweler.

THE ENGINEER WHO DESIGNS
RAILWAYS *by Arthur Mellen Wellington*

1   It would be well if engineering were less generally thought of, and even defined, as the art of constructing. In a certain im-

Arthur Mellen Wellington, *The Economic Theory of the Location of Railways* (New York, 1887).

portant sense it is rather the art of not constructing; or, to define it rudely but not inaptly, it is the art of doing that well with one dollar, which any bungler can do with two after a fashion.

2   There are, indeed, certain great triumphs of engineering genius—the locomotive, the truss bridge, the steel rail—which so rude a definition does not cover, for the bungler cannot attempt them at all; but such are rather invention than engineering proper. There is also in some branches of engineering, as in bridge-building, a certain other side to it, not covered by such a definition, which consists in doing that safely, at some cost or other which the bungler is likely to try to do and fail. He, therefore, in such branches, who is simply able to design a structure which will not fall down, may doubtless in some measure be called an engineer, although certainly not one of a very high type.

3   But to such engineering as is needed for laying out railways, at least, the definition given is literally applicable, for the economic problem is all there is to it. The ill-designed bridge breaks down; the ill-designed dam gives way; the ill-designed boiler explodes; the badly built tunnel caves in, and the bungler's bungling is betrayed. But a little practice and a little study of field geometry will enable any one of ordinary intelligence, without any engineering knowledge whatever in the larger sense, to lay out a railway from almost anywhere to anywhere, which will carry the locomotive with perfect safety, and perhaps show no obtrusive defects under what is too often the only test—inspection after construction from the rear end of a palace-car. Thus, for such work, the healthful checks which reveal the bungler's errors to the world and to himself do not exist. Nature, unhappily, has provided no way for the locomotive . . . to refuse to pass over an ill-designed railway as it refuses to pass over an ill-defined bridge.

4   Therefore, since there is no natural line between safety and danger to mark even so rude a distinction as that between the utterly bad and the barely tolerable, in the kind of engineering work we are to study, one may fairly say that the locating engineer has but the one end before him to justify his existence as such—to get the most value for a dollar which nature permits; and but one failure to fear—that he will not do so. Except as his work necessarily involves the preliminary design of constructive details, he has no lives to save or imperil; and the young engineer

cannot too early nor too forcibly have it impressed upon his mind that it takes no skill worth speaking of to do such work after a fashion, unless in the comparatively few localities (rare indeed in the United States) where to get a reasonable line of any kind is something of a feat. His true function and excuse for being as an engineer, as distinguished from a skilled workman, begins and ends in comprehending and striking a just balance between topographical possibilities, first cost, and future revenues and operating expenses.

Study Questions

ORGANIZATION AND CONTENT

1. Wellington's book, *The Economic Theory of the Location of Railways* (New York, 1887), was the first major American engineering work with literary quality. For what reason might we say that the first paragraph is intended to stimulate the reader's interest, or ideas?
2. Note that in both paragraphs 1 and 2 the author emphasizes the negative. What two aspects of engineering are ruled out of the definition in paragraph 2?
3. By what transition does the author take the reader to the positive aspect of his definition in paragraph 3? To what extent is the negative aspect still being expressed in paragraph 3?
4. What does the author mean by "healthful checks" in sentence 4, paragraph 3?
5. Judging by paragraph 4, how should you complete the following definition? "Railway engineering is . . ."
6. In what respects does Wellington's definition of railway engineering agree with Dr. Brennan's definition of civil engineering? What factor of engineering does Wellington introduce and emphasize that Dr. Brennan does not mention?

SENTENCE STRUCTURE

1. Explain why the pattern of sentence 2, paragraph 3, is especially good for giving vigorous emphasis to the author's ideas.
2. The author uses several transitional words; point out four and explain how they function.
3. In paragraph 4, sentence 1, the author mentions "one end" and "one failure," and explains what they are. For what grammatical purpose does he use the semicolon and the two dashes in the sentence?

4. The last clause of sentence 1, paragraph 2, begins with *but;* two sentences of paragraph 3 also begin with *but.* Why does the author begin them thus?

DICTION

1. Look up *literally, obtrusive, tolerable, topographical.*
2. What are their roots, and from what languages do they come?
3. What is the difference between *obtrude, intrude,* and *extrude?*

ASSIGNMENT

Begin exactly as Wellington does: "It would be well if _____ were less generally thought of as . . ." and put in the blank one of the following terms: (1) cooking, (2) attending college, (3) writing themes, (4) dancing, (5) business, (6) painting, (7) pharmacy, (8) literature, (9) sewing, (10) farming. Write a definition of the term in which you first stress the negative: that is, show how a certain concept is false or inadequate —and then, in a second paragraph, explain what a more accurate or more significant concept is.

A FAIRY STORY
by W. H. Auden

1   A fairy story, as distinct from a merry tale, or an animal story, is a serious tale with a human hero and a happy ending. The progression of its hero is the reverse of the tragic hero's: at the beginning he is either socially obscure or despised as being stupid or untalented, lacking in the heroic virtues, but at the end, he has surprised everyone by demonstrating his heroism and winning fame, riches, and love. Though ultimately he succeeds, he does not do so without a struggle in which his success is in doubt, for opposed to him are not only natural difficulties like glass mountains, or barriers of flame, but also hostile wicked powers, stepmothers, jealous brothers, and witches. In many cases, indeed, he would fail were he not assisted by friendly

From the Introduction, by W. H. Auden, to *Tales of Grimm and Andersen.* Copyright 1952, by W. H. Auden. Reprinted by permission of Random House, Inc.

powers who give him instructions or perform tasks for him which he cannot do himself; that is, in addition to his own powers, he needs luck, but this luck is not fortuitous but dependent upon his character and his actions. The tale ends with the establishment of justice; not only are the good rewarded but also the evil are punished.

2   Take, for example, "The Water of Life." Three brothers set out in turn on a difficult quest, to find the water of life to restore the King, their sick father, to health. Each one meets a dwarf who asks him where he is going. The two elder give rude answers and are punished by being imprisoned in ravines. The third brother gives a courteous answer and is rewarded by being told where the water of life is and how to appease the lions who guard it, but is warned to leave before the clock strikes twelve. He reaches the enchanted castle, where he finds a Princess who tells him to return in a year and marry her. At this point he almost fails because he falls asleep and only just manages to escape as the clock strikes twelve and the iron door shuts, carrying away a piece of his heel. On the way home he again meets the dwarf and begs him to release his brothers, which he does with a warning that they have bad hearts. The brothers steal the water of life from him and substitute salt water so that his father condemns him to be secretly shot. The huntsman entrusted with the task has not the heart to do it, and lets the young Prince go away into the forest. Now begins a second quest for the Princess. She has built a golden road to test her suitors. Whoever rides straight up it is to be admitted, whoever rides to the side is not. When the two elder brothers come to it they think "It would be a sin and a shame to ride over that" and so fail the test. At the end of the year, the exiled brother rides thither but is so preoccupied with thinking of the Princess that he never notices the golden road and rides straight up. They are married, the King learns how the elder brothers had betrayed the Prince, and they, to escape punishment, put to sea and never come back.

3   The hero is in the third or inferior position. (The youngest son inherits least.) There are two quests, each involving a test which the hero passes and his brothers fail.

4   The first test is the encounter with the dwarf. The elder brothers disregard him (a) because he looks like the last person

on earth who could help them, (b) they are impatient and thinking only of their success, and (c) what is wrong with their concentration on their task is, firstly, over-confidence in their own powers and, secondly, the selfishness of their motive. They do not really love their father but want him to reward them.

⁵ The hero, on the other hand, is (a) humble enough, (b) cares enough for his father's recovery, and (c) has a loving disposition toward all men, so that he asks the dwarf for assistance and gets it.

⁶ The second test of the golden road is a reversal of the first: the right thing to do this time is to take no notice of it. The brothers who dismissed the dwarf notice the road because of its worldly value, which is more to them than any Princess, while the hero, who paid attention to the dwarf, ignores the road because he is truly in love.

⁷ The Water of Life and the Princess are guarded by lions; these, in this tale, are not malevolent but ensure that no one shall succeed who has not learned the true way. The hero almost fails here by forgetting the dwarf's warning and falling asleep; further it is through falling asleep and not watching his brothers that they almost succeed in destroying him. The readiness to fall asleep is a sign of the trustfulness and lack of fear which are the qualities which bring about his success; at the same time it is pointed out that, carried too far, they are a danger to him.

Study Questions

ORGANIZATION AND CONTENT

1. In what class of things does the author place the term *fairy story?*
2. According to sentence 1, what differences exist between a fairy story and other kinds of stories?
3. We can hardly take sentence 1 as a sufficient definition. What other main differences should be added from the rest of paragraph 1? What contrasting situation of a tragic hero is implied in sentence 2?
4. What is the relation of paragraph 2 to paragraph 1?
5. Does "The Water of Life" meet all the requirements laid down for the fairy story in paragraph 1?

6. What is the main problem in organizing the material of paragraph 2?
7. To what extent does the interpretation in paragraphs 3–7 help in defining the term?
8. Point out how the author has used analysis in paragraphs 3, 4, 5, and 6.

SENTENCE STRUCTURE

1. What is the function of the colon in sentence 2, paragraph 1? In what other sentence is a colon used? Why? Does paragraph 1 or paragraph 2 have the longer sentences?
2. What is the likely reason why the average sentence length of the one paragraph is so much less than that of the other?
3. In the sentences of paragraphs 1, 4, 5, and 6 the author uses much parallel structure. Point it out, and explain why it is especially suitable in these paragraphs.
4. In sentence 2 of paragraph 6 which words receive chief emphasis?
5. Explain how sentence structure functions in terms of contrasts which are important in paragraph 7.

DICTION

1. Look up the meanings and learn the roots of the following words: *demonstrate, ultimately, fortuitous, quest, appease, encounter, malevolent.*
2. Is there a difference between *ultimately* and *lastly, fortuitous* and *accidental, malevolent* and *malicious?*
3. Explain how *appease* and *pacify* can come from the same root.
4. What are the differences among *quest, question, query, inquest, inquiry, inquisition?*

ASSIGNMENT

Write a definition in three paragraphs of a fable or a joke. In the first paragraph, classify the term and show how it differs from other things in the same class. In the second paragraph, summarize a fable or tell a good joke to illustrate the basic definition. In the third paragraph, interpret your example in terms of the requirements you laid down in paragraph 1.

HISTORY
by *Thomas Arnold*

1   The general idea of history seems to be, that it is the biography of a society. It does not appear to me to be history at all, but simply biography, unless it finds in the persons who are its subject something of a common purpose, the accomplishment of which is the object of their common life. History is to this common life of many, what biography is to the life of an individual. Take, for instance, any common family, and its members are soon so scattered from one another, and are engaged in such different pursuits, that although it is possible to write the biography of each individual, yet there can be no such thing, properly speaking, as the history of the family. But suppose all the members to be thrown together in one place, amidst strangers or savages, and there immediately becomes a common life,—a unity of action,—interest, and purpose, distinct from others around them, which renders them at once a fit subject of history. Perhaps I ought not to press the word "purpose"; because purpose implies consciousness in the purposer, and a society may exist without being fully conscious of its own business as a society. But whether consciously or not, every society—so much is implied in the very word—must have in it something of community; and so far as the members of it are members, so far as they are each incomplete parts, but taken together form a whole, so far, it appears to me, their joint life is the proper subject of history.

2   Accordingly we find the term history often applied to small and subordinate societies. We speak of the history of literary or scientific societies; we have histories of commercial bodies; histories of religious orders; histories of universities. In all these cases, history has to do with that which the several members of each of these societies have in common; it is, as I said, the biography of their common life. And it seems to me that it could not perform its office, if it had no distinct notion in what this common life consisted.

Thomas Arnold, *Introductory Lectures on Modern History* (New York, 1845).

Study Questions

1. Point out how Dr. Arnold has gone through the two steps necessary to a definition.
2. What contrasting terms, essential to his definition, does the author stress in sentences 1, 2, and 3?
3. In sentence 4 the author begins: "Take, for instance . . ." How does his *instance* help the reader to understand something significant about history?
4. In the first half of paragraph 1, what adjective is a key term? In the latter part of the paragraph, the function of this adjective is taken over by what noun? How early in the paragraph did that noun appear?
5. How does paragraph 2 contribute to the author's main thesis about history?
6. What terms used in paragraph 1 are repeated in paragraph 2?

SENTENCE STRUCTURE

1. In how many sentences does the word *history* appear? In which sentences does it have an emphatic position?
2. The author mentions himself several times; how does he introduce these personal references? Do they sound modest or egotistical?
3. Which sentences contain "interrupters"—parts set off by commas or dashes? Do they make the paragraphs seem smooth or choppy?
4. What determined the pattern of construction of sentence 2 of paragraph 2?

DICTION

1. Look up and find the roots of *biography, society, distinct, consciousness, community, subordinate, several.*
2. Why does the author use *consist in* instead of *consist of* in the last sentence?
3. Point out the "signal words"—like *but*—which give smooth transitions in these paragraphs.

ASSIGNMENT

Dr. Arnold illustrated his ideas about the meaning of history with an example of a family. Your problem is to explain your

ideas about the meaning of some term with the help of an illustration. Select one of these terms: love, justice, science, society,
or business.

HISTORY AND SOCIOLOGY
by Fred Morrow Fling

1   What is history? Unlike Bacon's "jesting Pilate," who asked,
"What is truth" and "would not stay for an answer," the historian
must tarry and answer the question he has raised. Turning the
pages of a history of the world, we note that it deals with all
man's social activities, economic, political, educational, artistic,
and religious. It describes them, however, not in a state of repose,
but of movement and change. In this change, our attention is
drawn, not to what repeats itself, but to what is new, to what
has never happened before and what can never happen again in
the same way. From all this it is evident that the historian is concerned with tracing *the unique evolution of man in his activities
as a social being*, the unique life record of humanity. If this be
history, then history cannot "repeat itself"; there cannot be "historical laws," for law is a generalization and a generalization assumes repetition.

2   It is clear, then, that *history deals with past social facts*, but
it is important to note that *all past social facts are not necessarily
historical facts*. The terms historical and social are not synonymous. A past social fact becomes an historical fact when it has
been made a part of an historical synthesis, for *historical, when
applied to human affairs, signifies nothing less than a certain logical way of looking at and organizing past social facts*. When our
attention is directed toward the *uniqueness*, the *individuality* of
past social facts, when they interest because of their importance
for the *unique evolution of man in his activities as a social being*,
in selecting the facts and grouping them into a complex, evolving
whole, we employ the historical method; the result of our work
is history.

Fred Morrow Fling, *The Writing of History* (New Haven, Yale
University Press, 1920).

³ If, on the contrary, we are interested in *what past social facts have in common*, in the way in which *social facts repeat themselves*, if our purpose is to form *generalizations*, or *laws* concerning social activities, we employ another logical method, the method of the natural science. We select our facts not for their individuality or for the importance of their individuality for a complex whole, but for what each fact has in common with others and *the synthesis is not a complex, unique whole, but a generalization in which no trace of the individuality of the past social fact remains*. The result of our work is sociology, not history. . . .

⁴ *Sociology cannot, then, be the science of history; it is the natural science of society.* Both the historians and the sociologists deal with past social facts, but not always with the same past social facts, nor in selecting and grouping the facts do they employ the same methods. *Their methods are logically different, because their ends are different.* This difference between the synthesis of history and that of sociology, or the natural science of society, may be crudely illustrated by a figure. Before us, upon a table, lie a large number of pieces of colorful glass in different sizes, shapes, and colors. The problem is to form from these fragments a single sheet of glass the size of the table top. It may be solved in two ways. The pieces may be thrown into a melting pot and when completely fused the molten glass may be poured into a mould the size of the table top. The individual pieces, however, have disappeared. In vain we look for the bit of orange or crimson of peculiar shape; it has lost its individuality in a composite whole. But there is another way of solving the problem of unity. Bit by bit the fragments might be fitted together until each piece has found its place and a complex whole, a stained-glass window, has been called into being. The pieces have not lost their individuality, but have retained it as parts of a larger, complex, unique whole. The first process is that of natural science, of sociology; the second, that of history.

Study Questions

ORGANIZATION AND CONTENT

1. How is Fling's definition of history in paragraph 1 similar to Dr. Arnold's definition?
2. What new idea is added that makes it different?
3. What is the basis of the distinction made between history and sociology?
4. Explain what is accomplished by the last sentence of paragraphs 1, 2, and 3.
5. Is it necessary, or not, that paragraph 3 follow paragraph 2?
6. Much of paragraph 4 is devoted to an analogy, that is, a partial similarity between things that makes it possible to set up a comparison. In his analogy involving the glass table top, what is the author actually comparing?
7. Which sentence of paragraph 3 probably started the author to thinking of the analogy?
8. The author says that the problem "may be solved in two ways." What do you expect after this statement? Explain how the author solved the problem of giving the reader what he expected at this point.
9. Suggest somewhat different ways of solving the problem. Do you think the author's solution is satisfactory?
10. If *sociology* is placed in the class of natural science, in what class should the term *history* be placed? Does the author indicate precisely in what class it belongs?

SENTENCE STRUCTURE

1. Sentence 3 ends with five adjectives. Are they arranged in any particular order?
2. Sentences 4–7 all have some repetition of ideas, mostly by the use of appositives. Point out appositives in these sentences. What is the effect of the appositives?
3. In which of these sentences does the author contrast a negative and a positive? How does he do it?
4. What similarity do you notice in the structure of the last sentence of paragraph 2 and the first sentence of paragraph 3?
5. What is the reason for this similarity?
6. Note how sentences of paragraph 4 are linked by repetitions of terms or by closely similar terms. Show the connection in this way of sentences 2, 3, and 4 each with the preceding sentence.

DICTION

1. The vocabulary here is not difficult; but two words are extremely important in the author's explanation: *unique* and *synthesis*. Look them up; be certain you know exactly what they mean. Why are they important?
2. Look up the roots of *evolution, repetition, complex, composite.*
3. Does the nature of his subject compel the author to use abstract diction?

ASSIGNMENT

In two or three paragraphs write definitions of two terms that may have something in common, yet also have some clear differences. Show what the differences are; try to use an analogy to illustrate them. Write on one of the following pairs:

1. Justice-love
2. Religion-ethics
3. Scientist-artist
4. Farmer-scientist
5. Business-profession

6. Science-technology
7. Athletics-game
8. Sociology-anthropology
9. Law-custom
10. Law-justice

CIVILIZATION
by *Winston S. Churchill*

1   There are few words which are used more loosely than the word "Civilization." What does it mean? It means a society based upon the opinion of civilians. It means that violence, the rule of warriors and despotic chiefs, the conditions of camps and warfare, of riot and tyranny, give place to parliaments where laws are made, and independent courts of justice in which over long periods those laws are maintained. That is Civilization—and in its soil grow continually freedom, comfort and culture. When Civilization reigns in any country, a wider and less harassed life is afforded to the masses of the people. The traditions of the past are cherished, and the inheritance bequeathed to us by former

wise or valiant men becomes a rich estate to be enjoyed and used by all.

2   The central principle of Civilization is the subordination of the ruling authority to the settled customs of the people and to their will as expressed through the Constitution. In this Island we have today achieved in a high degree the blessings of Civilization. There is freedom; there is law; there is love of country; there is a great measure of good will between classes; there is a widening prosperity. There are unmeasured opportunities of correcting abuses and making further progress.

Study Questions

ORGANIZATION AND CONTENT

1. Into what class does the author put the term *civilization?*
2. What does he say about the differences that set this term off from other members of the same class?
3. What term in sentence 4 contrasts with *civilians* in sentence 3?
4. What is the subject of *give* in sentence 4?
5. What is the relation of sentence 6 to sentence 5? Of sentence 7 to sentence 6?
6. Explain the usefulness, in the explanation, of the metaphor of the "rich estate" in sentence 7.
7. How is the first sentence of paragraph 2 related to ideas in paragraph 1?
8. Sentence 3 of paragraph 2 is related particularly to what word of sentence 2?
9. Why is the idea of sentence 4 of paragraph 2 not included in sentence 3, and what does sentence 4 contribute to the definition?

SENTENCE STRUCTURE

1. In paragraph 1 what words are repeated in sentences 2, 3, and 4 to provide links of transition?
2. By what means does the author expand the idea of "violence" in sentence 4?
3. In the second half of sentence 4 what terms balance terms in the first half?
4. What effect is gained by the unusual order of words in sentence 5?

5. Why does sentence 3 of paragraph 2 require four semicolons? Would the sentence be improved if it were shortened?

1. Look up *civic, civil, civilian.* What root appears in all three words?
2. Look up the origins of *despotic, tyranny, parliament.*
3. Is the vocabulary of the definition mostly abstract or mostly concrete? Point out examples of both kinds of terms.

Write a one-paragraph definition of tyranny, comfort, prosperity, or progress. Try to show both positive and negative aspects of the term.

CIVILIZATION
by Clive Bell

1 I have not yet defined civilization; but perhaps I have made definition superfluous. Any one, I fancy, who has done me the honour of reading so far will by now understand pretty well what I mean. Civilization is a characteristic of societies. In its crudest form it is the characteristic which differentiates what anthropologists call "advanced" from what they call "low" or "backward" societies. So soon as savages begin to apply reason to instinct, so soon as they acquire a rudimentary sense of values—so soon, that is, as they begin to distinguish between ends and means, or between direct means to good and remote—they have taken the first step upward. The first step towards civilization is the correcting of instinct by reason: the second, the deliberate rejection of immediate satisfactions with a view to obtaining subtler. The hungry savage, when he catches a rabbit, eats it there and then, or instinctively takes it home, as a fox might, to be eaten raw by his cubs; the first who, all hungry though he was, took it home and cooked it was on the road to Athens. He was a pioneer, who with equal justice may be described as the first decadent. The fact is significant. Civilization is something artificial and unnatural.

Clive Bell, *Civilization* (London, Chatto and Windus, 1928).

Progress and Decadence are interchangeable terms. All who have added to human knowledge and sensibility, and most of those even who have merely increased material comfort, have been hailed by contemporaries capable of profiting by their discoveries as benefactors, and denounced by all whom age, stupidity, or jealousy rendered incapable, as degenerates. It is silly to quarrel about words: let us agree that the habit of cooking one's victuals may with equal propriety be considered a step towards civilization or a falling away from the primitive perfection of the upstanding ape.

² From these primary qualities, Reasonableness and a Sense of Values, may spring a host of secondaries: a taste for truth and beauty, tolerance, intellectual honesty, fastidiousness, a sense of humour, good manners, curiosity, a dislike of vulgarity, brutality, and over-emphasis, freedom from superstition and prudery, a fearless acceptance of the good things of life, a desire for complete self-expression and for a liberal education, a contempt for utilitarianism and philistinism; in two words—sweetness and light. Not all societies that struggle out of barbarism grasp all or even most of these, and fewer still grasp any of them firmly. That is why we find a considerable number of civilized societies and very few highly civilized, for only by grasping a good handful of civilized qualities and holding them tight does a society become that.

Study Questions

ORGANIZATION AND CONTENT

1. The definition of civilization by Winston Churchill is part of a short speech entitled *Civilization;* that by Clive Bell is from a book entitled *Civilization.* These facts somewhat account for the different approaches that the two men take toward their topic. Does Bell place the term in the same class that Churchill used?
2. Using Bell's ideas, formulate a simple, one-sentence definition of civilization, showing precisely both class and differences.
3. Explain how the statements about the hungry savage help to explain the author's ideas about ends and means.
4. How can decadence possibly be a synonym for progress? Is this a paradox? How is paragraph 2 related to paragraph 1?
5. How has the author used analysis in making his definition?

6. Bell uses at least three terms that were used also by Churchill: *progress, comfort,* and *freedom.* Does he give them any different emphasis?

SENTENCE STRUCTURE

1. A few of Bell's sentences have only four or six words. Is there any reason why they should be so much shorter than the rest?
2. Explain the parallelism of sentence 5; of sentence 6.
3. Point out the contrasting elements of sentence 12.
4. What is the function of the colon in sentence 13? In paragraph 2, sentence 1?
5. What balanced ideas control the structure of the last two sentences?

DICTION

1. Look up *superfluous, anthropologists, rudimentary, decadent, sensibility, denounce, degenerates, fastidiousness, vulgarity, prudery, utilitarianism, philistinism, barbarism.*
2. In paragraph 1, sentence 7, the author uses a historical allusion. What does he mean by saying that the savage who cooked the rabbit was "on the road to Athens"?
3. Sentence 1 of paragraph 2 ends with "sweetness and light." It is another allusion; "Sweetness and Light" is the title of a chapter of Matthew Arnold's *Culture and Anarchy.* "Sweetness" means beauty, "light" means intelligence. Arnold also used the term philistinism; he called middle-class people Philistines—"enemies of the children of light." Why should he?
4. Is the vocabulary of this definition more concrete than that of the definition by Churchill?

ASSIGNMENT

1. Write a definition of *reasonableness.* Be sure to take both steps essential to good definition. Use at least two concrete examples to illustrate this abstraction.
2. How great a difference is there between *customs* and *traditions?* In one or two paragraphs explain how you would "draw the line" between them.
3. Do you or do you not believe that it is good to follow custom? Explain your position, largely by making use of a definition of custom.
4. Do you think that fastidiousness is good and vulgarity bad? Explain your position, making particular use of definition.

A CIVILIZATION
by Alan Houghton Brodrick

1   "Civilization" is what the psychologists call a "trigger-word" for it sets off a whole host of unreasoning and often unreasonable reactions. Since no technique has been devised for weighing one civilization against another, we cannot attach any clear meaning to the word "civilization" even if our latter day prophets drum into our ears that "civilization is in danger" for in the rich and varied, but meaningless propaganda-vocabulary of our time, the terms "civilization" and "civilized" are abstractions though useful enough to the polemist.

2   But if we cannot define "civilization," we can define "a civilization." The explanation is not, perhaps, very spectacular, but here it is. A civilization is a fairly complicated, complex and elaborate culture whose bearers (or some of them) know how to write.

3   A civilization, then, is a culture marked by the "presence" of script. The writing does not, of course, have to be the common possession of all those who live in the civilization's area. There are, even now, but few civilized communities all of whose members are fully literate, and in England 150 years ago most people could neither read nor write. In many ancient civilizations writing was practised by a small caste of priests and scribes. Letters were a mystery. The more elaborate is the culture or the civilization, the more layers and levels it contains. It is the fashion today to lump together, irrespective of their education, training and traditions, all the men and women who share the same sort of passport. Maybe we are moving towards the classless society, but we have not got to it yet, though we are not quite so far away from it as are the inhabitants of some countries of eastern Europe. All the same, the President of Harvard University is not in the same layer (of the United States civilization) as are the characters in "Tobacco Road."

4   A civilization is, then, a special form of a culture. But what is a culture?

5   But when the archaeologist and the anthropologist speak of

Alan Houghton Brodrick, *The Tree of Human History* (New York, Philosophical Library, 1952).

a "culture," two rather different meanings may be conveyed. The prehistorian (he is just a sort of archaeologist) talks of a "culture" and refers to a collection of man-made objects from which we may be able to deduce something about the ways of life and the ways of living of the people who fashioned the objects. The anthropologist means by a culture any form or pattern of human life as lived in a community.

6 We can, for the sake of convenience, sort out cultures as low, middling or high (though without making any judgment about spiritual or even aesthetic values) according as they show themselves to be more or less complicated, and what indicates whether a culture is low, middling or high, is the whole assemblage—arts and crafts, men's reaction to their surroundings, customs, traditions, ideas and religion—the more there is of it, so to speak, the "higher" the culture will be. Just one feature, such as profusion of gadgets and mechanical devices, is not alone enough to push the culture along to the position of "high." As Professor Coon has pointed out, the Aztecs had no metal-cutting tools but Aztec civilization was as elaborate as that of contemporary Hindus who forged excellent steel.

7 In the culture areas where we find civilizations eventually arising, the cultures are all fairly complex—generally speaking, we have domestic animals, permanent dwellings, pottery, tools of stone, wood and often metal. There is some form of art and there is evidence of religious cults.

Study Questions

ORGANIZATION AND CONTENT

1. The author is one of those "anthropologists" mentioned by Mr. Bell. Why is it that an anthropologist refuses to define *civilization* but says he can define *a civilization?*
2. In what class does the author place his term? What further attention does he feel obliged to give to the class?
3. How does the mention of the President of Harvard University in paragraph 3 help to explain the significance of elaborateness in culture?
4. *Tobacco Road* is a novel and a play. Why does the author allude to the characters of this work?

5. Paragraph 4, the shortest paragraph, is a transitional paragraph containing two parts. Explain how each part is related to other material.
6. How does the author make use of analysis in paragraphs 5 and 6?
7. Of what help is paragraph 7 in the definition?
8. How many specific places and people does the author mention? Is his explanation more specific than those of Churchill and Bell?

SENTENCE STRUCTURE

1. Sentences 1 and 2 contain clauses connected by the conjunction *for*. Explain why the author's thought in paragraph 1 requires this structure.
2. Sentence 1 of paragraph 2 is a complex sentence beginning with *but*. Is this a suitable sentence pattern here, or might the thought be better organized in some other sentence pattern?
3. Explain whether the other two sentences of paragraph 2 have effective structure.
4. Each of the first three sentences of paragraph 3 has an "interrupter," set off by commas. If the interrupters were left out, would the sentences be better or less good?
5. Sentence 7 of paragraph 3 also contains parenthetical material set off by commas. Why did the author place it where he did?
6. Sentence 1 of paragraph 6 is long and has several interruptive parts. Is the sentence too long? Too broken up with parenthetical material?
7. What is the effect of placing the dash before the last unit in this sentence and also in sentence 1 of paragraph 7? Would some other mark of punctuation be better?

DICTION

1. Look up *propaganda, abstractions, elaborate, polemist, literate, letters, archeologist, aesthetic, profusion, cult.*
2. What are the roots of *abstractions, archeologist, profusion, elaborate?*
3. Is the vocabulary of this selection chiefly formal or informal? Give evidence.

ASSIGNMENT

Write two paragraphs. In the first one show what common elements the three definitions of Churchill, Bell, and Brodrick have and also their differences. In the second one formulate a definition of civilization of your own. Try to make it more inclusive, or more significant, than any of the other three.

GENERAL AND SPECIAL EDUCATION
Report of the Harvard Committee

1   Education is broadly divided into general and special education; our topic now is the difference and the relationship between the two. The term, general education, is somewhat vague and colorless; it does not mean some airy education in knowledge in general (if there be such knowledge), nor does it mean education for all in the sense of universal education. It is used to indicate that part of a student's whole education which looks first of all to his life as a responsible human being and citizen; while the term, special education, indicates that part which looks to the student's competence in some occupation. These two sides of life are not entirely separable, and it would be false to imagine education for the one as quite distinct from education for the other—more will be said on this point presently. Clearly, general education has somewhat the meaning of liberal education, except that, by applying to high school as well as to college, it envisages immensely greater numbers of students and thus escapes the invidium which, rightly or wrongly, attaches to liberal education in the minds of some people. But if one clings to the root meaning of liberal as that which befits or helps to make free men, then general and liberal education have identical goals. The one may be thought of as an earlier stage of the other, similar in nature but less advanced in degree.

2   The very prevalence and power of the demand for special training makes doubly clear the need for a concurrent, balancing force in general education. Specialism enhances the centrifugal forces in society. The business of providing for the needs of

society breeds a great diversity of special occupations; and a given specialist does not speak the language of the other specialists. In order to discharge his duties as a citizen adequately, a person must somehow be able to grasp the complexities of life as a whole. Even from the point of view of economic success, specialism has its peculiar limitations. Specializing in a vocation makes for inflexibility in a world of fluid possibilities. Business demands minds capable of adjusting themselves to varying situations and of managing complex human institutions. Given the pace of economic progress, techniques alter speedily; and even the work in which the student has been trained may no longer be useful when he is ready to earn a living or soon after. Our conclusion, then, is that the aim of education should be to prepare an individual to become an expert both in some particular vocation or art and in the general art of the free man and the citizen. Thus the two kinds of education once given separately to different social classes must be given together to all alike.

³ In this epoch in which almost all of us must be experts in some field in order to make a living, general education therefore assumes a peculiar importance. Since no one can become an expert in all fields, everyone is compelled to trust the judgment of other people pretty thoroughly in most areas of activity. I must trust the advice of my doctor, my plumber, my lawyer, my radio repairman, and so on. Therefore I am in peculiar need of a kind of sagacity by which to distinguish the expert from the quack, and the better from the worse expert. From this point of view, the aim of general education may be defined as that of providing the broad critical sense by which to recognize competence in any field. William James said that an educated person knows a good man when he sees one. There are standards and a style for every type of activity—manual, athletic, intellectual, or artistic; and the educated man should be one who can tell sound from shoddy work in a field outside his own. General education is especially required in a democracy where the public elects its leaders and officials; the ordinary citizen must be discerning enough so that he will not be deceived by appearances and will elect the candidate who is wise in his field.

⁴ Special education comprises a wider field than vocationalism; and correspondingly, general education extends beyond the limits

of merely literary preoccupation. An example will make our point clearer. A scholar—let us say a scientist (whether student or teacher)—will, in the laudable aim of saving himself from narrowness, take a course in English literature, or perhaps read poetry and novels, or perhaps listen to good music and generally occupy himself with the fine arts. All this, while eminently fine and good, reveals a misapprehension. In his altogether unjustified humility, the scientist wrongly interprets the distinction between liberal and illiberal in terms of the distinction between the humanities and the sciences. Plato and Cicero would have been very much surprised to hear that geometry, astronomy, and the sciences of nature in general, are excluded from the humanities. There is also implied a more serious contempt for the liberal arts, harking back to the fallacy which identifies liberal education with the aristocratic ideal. The implication is that liberal education is something only genteel. A similar error is evident in the student's attitude toward his required courses outside his major field as something to "get over with," so that he may engage in the business of serious education, identified in his mind with the field of concentration.

5   Now, a general education is distinguished from special education, not by subject matter, but in terms of method and outlook, no matter what the field. Literature, when studied in a technical fashion, gives rise to the special science of philology; there is also the highly specialized historical approach to painting. Specialism is interchangeable, not with natural science, but with the method of science, the method which abstracts material from its context and handles it in complete isolation. The reward of scientific method is the utmost degree of precision and exactness. But, as we have seen, specialism as an educational force has its own limitations; it does not usually provide an insight into general relationships.

6   It is most unfortunate if we envisage general education as something formless—that is to say, the taking of one course after another; and as something negative, namely, the study of what is not in a field of concentration. Just as we regard the courses in concentration as having definite relations to one another, so should we envisage general education as an organic whole whose parts join in expounding a ruling idea and in serving a common

aim. And to do so means to abandon the view that all fields and all departments are equally valuable vehicles of general education. It also implies some prescription. At the least it means abandoning the usual attitude of regarding "distribution" as a sphere in which the student exercises a virtually untrammeled freedom of choice. It may be objected that we are proposing to limit the liberty of the student in the very name of liberal education. Such an objection would only indicate an ambiguity in the conception of liberal education. We must distinguish between liberalism in education and education in liberalism. The former, based as it is on the doctrine of individualism, expresses the view that the student should be free in his choice of courses. But education in liberalism is an altogether different matter; it is education which has a pattern associated with the liberal outlook. In this view, there are truths which none can be free to ignore, if one is to have that wisdom through which life can become useful. These are the truths concerning the structure of the good life and concerning the factual conditions by which it may be achieved, truths comprising the goals of the free society.

Study Questions

ORGANIZATION AND CONTENT

1. This is a good example of definition that makes use of analysis; the definition begins with an act of analysis. Explain what it is.
2. What is the topic sentence of paragraph 1?
3. What is the relation of sentence 2 to sentences 1 and 3?
4. Explain the relation of the second half of sentence 3 to the first half.
5. What concession is made in sentence 4?
6. In sentence 5 what new term is introduced to help the explanation along? What advantage does this term evidently have?
7. Notice that along with the definition, there is an argument; as the definition is being gradually developed, an *argument for* general education is also being presented. What arguments for general education are presented in paragraphs 2 and 3? Enumerate them.

8. What main points are made in paragraphs 4 and 5?
9. In paragraph 6 some antagonism, or contradiction, between *liberalism* and *prescription* is emphasized. Why is it necessary to do so?
10. What has the idea of an "organic whole" (sentence 2) to do with the matter?
11. Why do the authors reject "liberalism in education" and favor "education in liberalism"?
12. What are the "truths which none can be free to ignore"?
13. What have they to do with the definition of general education?
14. Show how paragraph 6 and paragraph 2 are related in their talk of the free man and free society.

SENTENCE STRUCTURE

1. Point out the difference in sentence structure between sentences 1–4 and sentences 5–7.
2. Sentence 1 of paragraph 2 is interesting. Note how the subject with its modifiers is almost exactly balanced by the predicate with its modifiers. Explain this balance in more detail.
3. Suppose that the subordinate elements which begin sentences 1 and 2 of paragraph 3 were switched to a position after the main clause; what would be the result? Would the sentences be better or less good?
4. What is the function of the semicolons in the last two sentences of paragraph 3?
5. What is the sentence pattern of sentence 1 of paragraph 4? Is it reasonable that the material should be organized according to this pattern?
6. Is the thought of sentence 2 of paragraph 4 worth a whole separate sentence?
7. Do sentences 3 and 4 of paragraph 4 contain too many interruptive commas and dashes?
8. Sentence 2 of paragraph 5 begins with the word *literature* and ends with the word *painting*. Is this a suitable arrangement, or would the sentence be improved if these words were shifted to other positions? (Suppose, for example, that *literature* came just before the semicolon; or just after the *when*-clause; or that *painting* came just after the semicolon; or that *literature* and *painting* were both in the same main clause.)

DICTION

1. Look up the following words and learn the roots from which they originally come: *invidium, prevalence, concurrent, centrifugal, diversity, inflexibility, manual, athletic, intellectual, artistic, preoccupation, laudable, humanities, fallacy, aristocratic, genteel, philology, prescription, ambiguity.*
2. For each of these words give another word based on the same root.
3. The vocabulary of this definition is largely abstract and general. Can you find as many as ten words that are concrete?

ASSIGNMENT

Write a one-paragraph definition of an expert or a specialist; or of vocationalism or general education. Use some illustrations —examples or analogies—to help make your meaning clear.

AN AMERICAN
by J. Hector St. John de Crevecoeur

What then is the American, this new man? He is either an European, or the descendant of an European, hence that strange mixture of blood, which you will find in no other country. I could point out to you a family whose grandfather was an Englishman, whose wife was Dutch, whose son married a French woman, and whose present four sons have now four wives of different nations. He is an American, who, leaving behind him all his ancient prejudices and manners, receives new ones from the new mode of life he has embraced, the new government he obeys, and the new rank he holds. He becomes an American by being received in the broad lap of our great *Alma Mater.* Here individuals of all nations are melted into a new race of men, whose labours and posterity will one day cause great changes in the world. Americans are the western pilgrims, who are carrying along with them that great mass of arts, sciences, vigour, and industry which began long since in the east; they will finish the

J. Hector St. John de Crevecoeur, *Letters from an American Farmer* (1782).

great circle. The Americans were once scattered all over Europe; here they are incorporated into one of the finest systems of population which has ever appeared, and which will hereafter become distinct by the power of the different climates they inhabit. The American ought therefore to love this country much better than that wherein either he or his forefathers were born. Here the rewards of his industry follow with equal steps the progress of his labour; his labour is founded on the basis of nature, *self-interest;* can it want a stronger allurement? Wives and children, who before in vain demanded of him a morsel of bread, now, fat and frolicsome, gladly help their father to clear those fields whence exuberant crops are to arise to feed and to clothe them all; without any part being claimed, either by a despotic prince, a rich abbot, or a mighty lord. Here religion demands but little of him; a small voluntary salary to the minister, and gratitude to God; can he refuse these? The American is a new man, who acts upon new principles; he must therefore entertain new ideas, and form new opinions. From involuntary idleness, servile dependence, penury, and useful labour, he has passed to toils of a very different nature, rewarded by ample subsistence.—This is an American.

Study Questions

ORGANIZATION AND CONTENT

1. Crevecoeur (1735–1813), the author of the definition of an American, belonged by birth to the lesser nobility of Normandy. He served in the French forces under Montcalm from about 1755 to 1760, came to the British Colonies, and was naturalized in New York in 1764. His *Letters from an American Farmer* (1782) were based on his travels and on his experiences as the owner of farms in New York and New Jersey in pre-Revolutionary days. The American, then, of whom he writes, "this new man," is the American of the eighteenth century before there was a nation called the United States of America. What evidence does the author give that the American is a "new man"?
2. What is the function of sentence 3 in the explanation?
3. If Americans are pilgrims, what sort of pilgrimage are they making?

4. How has the American become different from his European brothers or grandfathers?
5. What is the particularly American attitude regarding labor, agriculture, marriage, religion?
6. Explain how the last three sentences are related to the discussion which precedes them.
7. Put the essential idea of Crevecoeur into a one-sentence definition of an American.

SENTENCE STRUCTURE

1. Sentence 4 has both parallel structure and repetition of words. Point them out.
2. Why are parallel structure and repetition effective in sentence 4?
3. At least half the sentences of this paragraph contain the word *American* or *Americans.* Consider why these words are so often repeated and the emphasis they receive in their positions in the sentences where they appear.
4. Several clauses begin with *here.* Explain what particular emphasis *here* has in those clauses.

DICTION

1. Look up *prejudices, manners, Alma Mater, posterity, incorporate, allurement, exuberant, servile, penury.*
2. What other words are based on the same roots as *prejudices, incorporate, servile?*
3. Crevecoeur says that the American works because the basis of nature is self-interest. *Nature* is an important and difficult term; it has been used in many different senses. What meaning does the author intend it to have?

ASSIGNMENT

An American is a man who acts in a certain way. Similarly, as was stated earlier, a hero is a man acting in a certain way. Write a definition of a hero, showing how the way in which a hero acts is different from the way of all other persons. Take into account the following questions:

1. Must a hero undergo some kind of test?
2. Must he be involved in a struggle and incur some risk?
3. Must he do something out of the ordinary?
4. Must he show courage?

5. Must he do something for the good of others?
6. Can a person be a hero if he merely does what he is ordered to do or if he himself feels no danger?
7. Must he succeed in his undertakings, or is failure permissible?
8. Can he be a hero if no one knows about his acts?

You will no doubt find that specific examples will help you to communicate your ideas.

THE SPIRIT OF LIBERTY
by Justice Learned Hand

1   We have gathered here to affirm a faith, a faith in a common purpose, a common conviction, a common devotion. Some of us have chosen America as the land of our adoption; the rest have come from those who did the same. For this reason we have some right to consider ourselves a picked group, a group of those who had the courage to break from the past and brave the dangers and the loneliness of a strange land.

2   What was the object that nerved us, or those who went before us, to this choice? We sought liberty: freedom from oppression, freedom from want, freedom to be ourselves. This we then sought. This we now believe that we are by way of winning.

3   What do we mean when we say that first of all we seek liberty? I often wonder whether we do not rest our hopes too much upon constitutions, upon laws and upon courts. These are false hopes; believe me, these are false hopes. Liberty lives in the hearts of men and women. When it dies there, no constitution, no law, no court can save it. No constitution, no law, no court can even do much to help it. While it lives there, it needs no constitution, no law, no court to save it.

4   And what is this liberty which must live in the hearts of men and women? It is not the ruthless, the unbridled will. It is not freedom to do as one likes. That is the denial of liberty, and leads straight to its overthrow. A society in which men recognize no check upon their freedom, soon becomes a society where free-

Reprinted by permission of *The New York Times*. Published July 2, 1944.

dom is the possession of only a savage few; as we have learned to our sorrow.

⁵ What then is the spirit of liberty? I cannot define it; I can only tell you my own faith. The spirit of liberty is the spirit which is not too sure that it is right. The spirit of liberty is the spirit which seeks to understand the minds of other men and women. The spirit of liberty is the spirit which weighs their interests alongside its own without bias. The spirit of liberty remembers that not even a sparrow falls to earth unheeded. The spirit of liberty is the spirit of Him, who, near 2,000 years ago, taught mankind that lesson it has never learned, but has never quite forgotten; that there may be a kingdom where the least shall be heard and considered side by side with the greatest.

⁶ And now in that spirit, that spirit of America which has never been, and which may never be; nay, which never will be, except as the conscience and the courage of Americans create it; yet in the spirit of that America which lies hidden in some form in the aspirations of us all; in the spirit of that America for which our young men are at this moment fighting and dying; in that spirit of liberty and of America I ask you to rise and with me to pledge our faith in the glorious destiny of our beloved country: "I pledge allegiance to the flag of the United States of America and to the Republic for which it stands—one nation indivisible, with liberty and justice for all."

Study Questions

ORGANIZATION AND CONTENT

On May 21, 1944, Justice Hand of the United States Circuit Court of Appeals made this speech in Central Park, New York City, when American citizenship was being awarded to 150,000 newly naturalized citizens. The United States at that time was at war. The speaker was addressing an audience of more than one million persons. His main purpose was not to give a definition but to speak in an inspiring way on a patriotic occasion. But the speech is a good example of how definition may be used in connection with other purposes.

It is worth while to pay some attention to the problem that the speaker faced. (1) The speech had to end with the pledge to the flag. (2) It could not be very long. (3) It must have some connection with the pledge. (4) It must interest both citizens of long standing, who had often heard the pledge and perhaps thought it trite, and the newly naturalized ones, to many of whom the pledge was a new thing; somehow the pledge to the flag must be made to seem significant to both groups.

1. The speech is divided into three parts: I. paragraphs 1 and 2; II. paragraphs 3, 4, and 5; III. paragraph 6. After answering the other questions on organization and content, explain how this pattern of organization is related to the problem of the speaker.
2. In paragraphs 1 and 2 *we* and *us* appear nine times. What noun (or nouns) do these pronouns represent?
3. The speaker insists that "we" have things in "common." Which part of the pledge to the flag does this idea refer to?
4. First of all, the speaker says, "we sought liberty." To what questions of definition is he then led?
5. In paragraph 3 liberty is treated mostly in a negative way. Instead of living in the political structure of a nation, liberty lives where?
6. In paragraph 4 the speaker also tells us where liberty *is not*. If liberty is not freedom to do as one likes, what instruments must society then use to help preserve liberty?
7. In its treatment of liberty paragraph 5 sets up a kind of golden mean between extremes of individualism and of dependence upon political machinery. What relation then does paragraph 5 have with paragraphs 3 and 4?
8. In his definition of the spirit of liberty the author says that it weighs the interests of others alongside its own without bias. What aspect of the pledge to the flag does this idea represent?
9. Judging by paragraph 5, what ethical tradition has especially influenced the thoughts and feelings of the author?
10. The author says that he cannot define the spirit of liberty; yet he gives a kind of definition of it. How does his definition differ from some of the other definitions you have studied?
11. In paragraph 6 the speaker asks the audience to pledge allegiance in "that spirit of an America which has never been." What does *America* then represent, as the speaker uses the term?

SENTENCE STRUCTURE

1. In each paragraph of the speech several words and phrases are repeated. Point them out.
2. Explain how grammatical parallelism is related to the repetition.

3. What is the effect of the repetition? What is the probable reason for it?
4. Which sentences are so constructed that they have a strong and fairly regular rhythm?

DICTION

1. Are there any words that you do not know?
2. Is the vocabulary of the speech mainly abstract and general or mainly concrete and particular?
3. Which portion is the most abstract; which portion is the most concrete?
4. Look up *alliteration.* Point out two examples where the author may have chosen a word because of its alliteration.
5. The value of this speech may lie more in its emotional force than in its intellectual keenness. Does its emotional force come from the connotations of the words more than from the rhythm of the sentences? (Consider, for example, the connotations of *sparrow* and *kingdom* in paragraph 5.) Do any other factors increase the emotional quality of the speech?

ASSIGNMENT

In one or two paragraphs write a definition of the American Cause or the American Dream or American Democracy or the American Educational Ideal or something ennobling like the Spirit of Beauty or the Spirit of Science. Imitate Justice Hand's method by repeating some of the key terms so as to achieve an emotional effect. However, do not become overemotional; keep the writing dignified.

COMPARISON AND CONTRAST

It has already been shown to some extent how writers use the principles of comparison and contrast in explaining meanings. Since definition requires the showing of differences among terms, some element of contrast naturally appears in definition and is indeed almost inevitable. The discussions of history and sociology, and of general and special education, in the section on definition could properly appear in this section.

Comparison and contrast are also used frequently in other

types of expository writing. Indeed, the human mind turns naturally and with ease to the locating of likenesses and differences. It is convenient to try to explain something unfamiliar by indicating how it resembles something familiar. The *how* will be brought out by producing evidence for the resemblance in the form of specific details. The details are illustrations of the main idea, that likeness exists. Thus, comparison and contrast as methods of exposition gain their effectiveness and power from their force as examples. The examples, that is, the particular details, are brought into view no doubt through an act of analysis.

The mind is impressed by differences as well as by similarities. If a person travels abroad, he will often be thinking: This is *not* the way we do it at home. Or when he inspects his personality, he discovers: "This is *not* the way I felt last year, or when I was a freshman, or when I was a child." Constantly, too, he is watching to see whether things turn out as they were forecast. "No," he tells the politician, "this is *not* what you promised; the state of affairs is different from what it should be." Since he has noticed a difference, he complains because one condition is less good than another that he hoped for. Contrast is often the basis of criticism and complaint; yet both contrast and comparison may be also the basis of praise. Whenever anything is judged, a standard is used; that is, the thing in question is compared with the standard. Therefore, one is very likely to turn to comparison and contrast when discussing anything in terms of standards of excellence. The selection on general and special education involves judgments of worth; so do the selections ahead on women before marriage and after marriage, on good and not good teachers, on American and British students, and on two kinds of literary criticism. Comparison and contrast have a special usefulness, then, for the bringing out of values.

The technique of presenting material according to these methods of exposition presents certain possibilities. Suppose two things, A and B, are being compared. The author may write one whole paragraph on A and a second paragraph on B. He might, using shorter paragraphs perhaps, do this and then continue with a third paragraph on A, a fourth on B, and so on alternately to the end. On the other hand, the writer might switch from A to B when halfway through the first paragraph and follow that half-paragraph pattern until he was finished. Clearly also one might write first one sentence about A, the next about B, and so forth, following a pattern of more rapid alternation. As will be seen by studying the models, each of these techniques offers advantages and creates certain effects.

✿ ✿ ✿

EDUCATED WOMEN BEFORE MARRIAGE AND AFTER MARRIAGE
by Adlai E. Stevenson

Now, as I have said, women, especially educated women such as you, have a unique opportunity to influence us, man and boy, and to play a direct part in the unfolding drama of our free society. But I am told that nowadays the young wife or mother is short of time for the subtle arts, that things are not what they used to be; that once immersed in the very pressing and particular problems of domesticity many women feel frustrated and far apart from the great issues and stirring debates for which their education has given them understanding and relish. Once they read Baudelaire. Now it is the *Consumers' Guide*. Once they wrote poetry. Now it's the laundry list. Once they discussed art and philosophy until late in the night. Now they are so tired they fall asleep as soon as the dishes are finished. There is, often, a sense of contraction, of closing horizons and lost opportunities. They had hoped to play their part in the crisis of the age. But what they do is wash the diapers.

Study Questions

ORGANIZATION AND CONTENT

1. This paragraph is a part of a Commencement Address that Adlai Stevenson gave at Smith College; therefore, the manner in which he speaks to his audience in sentence 1. *But*, a word of contrast, begins sentence 2. With what idea of sentence 1 does the idea of sentence 2 contrast?
2. What relation does sentence 9 have to the six preceding sentences?

From *What I Think* by Adlai E. Stevenson. Copyright 1956. Reprinted by permission of Harper & Row, Publishers.

3. What are the contrasting terms in sentences 10 and 11?
4. Would the paragraph be better if it closed with sentence 9? Or better if sentence 9 were placed at the end? Give reasons for your answer.

SENTENCE STRUCTURE

1. Note the variety of sentence length. How long is sentence 2? How long are the next half-dozen sentences?
2. In these sentences what repeated words provide the points of contrast?
3. Which of these half-dozen sentences sound more dignified? Which less dignified?
4. What is the effect of this contrast in tone?

DICTION

1. Look up *subtle, immersed, frustrated, Baudelaire.*
2. Does the author use any colloquial words or expressions?
3. Point out two examples of alliteration in sentence 2.
4. If the words that alliterate were replaced by nonalliterating words, would there be any change in effect?

ASSIGNMENT

Write a paragraph in which you contrast a hope and a reality; it might be in terms of anticipation and disappointment or of fear and delight. Such topics as dormitory life, a college course, a trip, a vacation, a friendship would be suitable. Use several short contrasting sentences like Stevenson's.

GOOD AND NOT GOOD TEACHERS
by Franz Schneider

1   No one can be a good teacher in our sense who is a religious escapist. As such he may be a good specialist in the fields of scholarship that are purely descriptive and lie far in the past, or he may be a good scientist who by dint of higher mathematics communes with the great power behind all visible phenomena. However, a good teacher, as we conceive him, never ceases to

Franz Schneider, *More than an Academic Question* (Berkeley, Calif., The Pestalozzi Press, 1945). Reprinted by permission of Franz Schneider.

think of his fellow beings, of their fates, and their sorrows; he is at all times eager to bring about a social structure wherein people shall be less cramped, more free.

2   Some teachers have the outward appearance of good teachers, but they are not, even though their students have no special fault to find with them. They are not good teachers such as the world needs, because they have no social vision, no social urge, no fight in them. They know their respective fields, they are men of orderly minds, and their courses are sensibly planned and efficiently executed. Yet, personally they are narrowly subject-minded, hold mankind in low esteem, even as regards the big mass of our college students, and consider anyone a fool who believes in the perfectibility of humankind on a large scale.

Study Questions

ORGANIZATION AND CONTENT

1. According to sentence 1 what disqualifies a person for good teaching?
2. In sentence 2 "a good specialist" and "a good scientist" are mentioned. How are these people different from "a good teacher," who is described in sentence 3?
3. Which particular not-good teachers are discussed in paragraph 2? In which sentence is this class of teachers introduced?
4. In sentence 2 of paragraph 2 certain lacks of not-good teachers are pointed out. What is the reader supposed to infer about the qualities of good teachers?
5. What does the author praise even in not-good teachers?
6. Why does he begin the last sentence with *yet?*

SENTENCE STRUCTURE

1. Sentence 2 is a balanced sentence. Which parts in the second half do not correspond exactly to parts in the first half?
2. Why is this sentence pattern suitable to the thought?
3. Sentence 3 has a more regular rhythm than sentence 2. What is there in the structure of the sentence that makes this so?
4. Is the rhythm of sentence 3 too regular and too evident?
5. The last three sentences of paragraph 2 all use parallel grammatical structures, each with three items. Identify each group of three in grammatical terms.

1. Look up *escapist, scientist, communes, phenomena.*
2. Some of the vocabulary in this selection is quite abstract. What specific examples can you suggest to bring out the meaning of "social vision" and "social urge" (sentence 2 of paragraph 2)?
3. In the light of the author's ideas, what three adjectives would best describe a good teacher?

ASSIGNMENT

Write a paragraph of about ten sentences in which you begin like Schneider—"No one can be a good . . ."—but substitute preacher, doctor, coach, farmer, mechanic, counselor, or musician for *teacher.* Use comparison and contrast, emphasizing the negative.

AMERICAN STUDENTS AND BRITISH STUDENTS *by J. Frank Dobie*

1 As far as quality of mind is concerned—and quality of mind is something that all the theories of democracy in the world cannot equalize—there is no detectable difference between top American students and top British students. The average student at the one English University I have acquaintance with is, however, better trained mentally, has the fibers in his mind better developed, enjoys the act of thinking more and has more intellectual curiosity than the average American student. He is more civilized, just as the average member of Parliament is more civilized than the average Congressman, less given to the puerile in thought, speech and conduct. He demonstrates how the charm of youthfulness may be added to by dignity and mental maturity. He gives a richer meaning to Wordsworth's "The child is father of the man."

2 Go back a few years before the war to any State University in America. The first class of the morning is over. Students make a rush for breakfast or for coffee or maybe only for some form

From *A Texan in England* by J. Frank Dobie. Reprinted by permission of Little, Brown & Company. Copyright 1944, 1945, by J. Frank Dobie.

of "pep" beverage at a drugstore near at hand. Those that are not talking are looking maybe at a newspaper. What are they looking at in the newspaper? Two things generally: sports or the funnies. Within the last fifteen years a much higher percentage of American students than formerly have come to take a serious interest in political, economic, social questions. But it is still a widespread idea among Americans who are not students, that amusement—entertainment—consists of something that will not require the constitutionally tired business man to exercise his brain. The tired businessman's brain is devoted to practical things, and it isn't fun to use it. Fun is something to be bought, through a nickelodeon, in a picture show, from the voices of radio wits, out of colored Sunday supplements and their weekday counterparts.

³ The English collegian, on the contrary, has no colored Sunday supplement. He follows sports, goes to cinemas, wouldn't stand for having the peace of his pub or his tea-house constantly violated by jazz music; he listens to ideas as well as opiates over the radio, and reads the editorials and reports on Parliamentary debates in his newspaper. His intellectual activity is not modeled on that of the tired businessman.

Study Questions

ORGANIZATION AND CONTENT

1. What class of college student is the author primarily discussing?
2. What is the function of sentence 1?
3. What "contrast-word" is significant in sentence 2?
4. Sentence 2 lists four ways in which certain British students are superior to certain American students. What are they?
5. In the rest of paragraph 1 the British student is praised for what other qualities?
6. What do the first six sentences of paragraph 2 accomplish?
7. What sort of objection is sentence 7 intended to meet?
8. According to paragraph 2 Americans largely expect to get "fun" by what means? And by what means do they *not* expect to get fun?
9. What is the relation of the second half of paragraph 2 to the first half?

10. According to paragraph 2 the American student is following what model? In the light of this discussion, is it fair to infer that his model is a bad one?
11. What contrast is brought out in paragraph 3?
12. What points of paragraph 1 is paragraph 3 intended to illustrate?
13. Though he is writing about college students, do you think that the author is actually contrasting British society and American society?
14. Do these three paragraphs have topic sentences? If so, what are they?

SENTENCE STRUCTURE

1. The beginning and the ending of a sentence are positions of emphasis. Contrast sentences 1 and 2 of paragraph 1 in terms of the material placed at the beginning and at the end.
2. Why do sentences 3, 4, and 5 all begin with *he?*
3. Does the material at the end of sentences 3, 4, and 5 have enough emphasis?
4. Contrast the structure of the first six sentences of paragraph 2 with that of the other four sentences in the remainder of that paragraph.

DICTION

1. Look up *puerile, cinema, pub, violate, opiate.*
2. In paragraph 1 is "more civilized" to be equated with "less given to the puerile"?
3. Point out colloquial diction. Is this colloquialism pleasing or not?
4. Does the author's "more civilized" fit one of the definitions of "civilization" that you have studied? Explain.

ASSIGNMENT

Write three similar paragraphs on one of the following topics contrasting:

1. Men students and women students
2. Cultured people and "tired businessmen"
3. Admirable young people and juvenile delinquents
4. Typical students in two different curricula

Follow Mr. Dobie's pattern of organization: that is, A, then B, then back to A.

SPIRIT OF INTELLECTUAL MOVEMENT AND SPIRIT OF POLITICAL AND RELIGIOUS MOVEMENT *by Thomas Arnold*

We might think, *a priori*, that the spirit of political, and that of religious movement, would go on together, each favouring and encouraging the other. But the spirit of intellectual movement differs from the other two in this, that it is comparatively one with which the mass of mankind have little sympathy. Political benefits all men can appreciate; and all good men, and a great many more than we might well dare to call good, can appreciate also the value not of all, but of some religious truth which to them may seem all: the way to obtain God's favour and to worship Him aright, is a thing which great bodies of men can value, and be moved to the most determined efforts, if they fancy that they are hindered from attaining to it. But intellectual movement in itself is a thing which few care for. Political truth may be dear to them, so far as it affects their common well-being; and religious truth so far as they may think it their duty to learn it; but truth abstractedly, and because it is truth, which is the object, I suppose, of the pure intellect, is to the mass of mankind a thing indifferent. Thus the workings of the intellect come even to be regarded with suspicion as unsettling: We have got, we say, what we want, and we are well contented with it; why should we be kept in perpetual restlessness, because you are searching after some new truths, which when found will compel us to derange the state of our minds in order to make room for them. Thus the democracy of Athens was afraid of and hated Socrates; and the poet who satirized Cleon, knew that Cleon's partisans no less than his own aristocratical friends would sympathize with his satire, when directed against the philosophers. But if this hold in political matters, much more does it hold religiously. The two great parties of the Christian world have each their own standard of truth by which they try all things: Scripture on the one hand, the voice of the church on the other. To both therefore the pure intellectual movement is not only unwelcome, but they dislike it. It will question what they will not allow to be questioned; it may arrive

Thomas Arnold, *Introductory Lectures on Modern History* (New York, 1845).

at conclusions which they would regard as impious. And therefore in an age of religious movement particularly, the spirit of intellectual movement soon finds itself proscribed rather than countenanced.

Study Questions

1. What is the basis of the contrast that the author makes between the spirit of intellectual movement and the spirit of political and religious movement? Why does he begin sentence 2 with *but?*
2. What term in sentence 2 is related to "favouring and encouraging" in sentence 1?
3. Sentence 3 is a long sentence with three parts; what phase of the matter being discussed is taken up in each part?
4. Why is sentence 4 a short sentence? What is the effect of its being short?
5. Which phase of the subject is taken up in each part of sentence 5? What explanation of "intellectual movement" is given in sentence 5? How is sentence 5 related to sentence 3?
6. Both sentence 6 and sentence 7 begin with *thus;* what does the word mean in each sentence?
7. The historical allusion in sentence 7 involves Socrates, a philosopher; Cleon, a leader of the masses; and Aristophanes, a comic poet. Which people of Athens would sympathize with Aristophanes' satirical attacks upon Cleon? And which with similar attacks upon Socrates? What does Socrates the philosopher have to do with intellectual movement?
8. In sentence 7 the spirit of intellectual movement is being contrasted with what? And with what in sentence 8? Point out the transitional function of sentence 8.
9. Sentences 9–12 are all devoted to what? With what reason in sentence 9 is the *therefore* of sentence 10 linked? With what reason in sentence 11 is the *therefore* of sentence 12 linked?

1. Explain the reason for the unusual word order in the first clause of sentence 3.
2. Could the material of sentence 4 just as well have been included in sentence 3?

3. Is sentence 5 a loose sentence, balanced sentence, or periodic sentence?
4. Why are the three parts of sentence 5 arranged in the order that they have?
5. Why is sentence 5 punctuated as it is?
6. How is the author able to end sentence 5 with an adjective?
7. What is the function of the colon in sentence 6? In sentence 9?
8. The author has organized sentence 10 so as to give special emphasis to what thought?
9. Point out parallel structure in sentence 11. Is the chief emphasis the same in both parts of sentence 11?

DICTION

1. From what language does *a priori* come? What does it mean? Why is it italicized?
2. Look up *indifferent, derange, democracy, satirize, partisan, philosopher, proscribe, countenance.*
3. Which of these words have roots that come from Latin? Which from Greek?

ASSIGNMENT

In the same manner that Dr. Arnold contrasts the reception of intellectual movement with that of political and religious movement, write a paragraph in which you contrast:

1. The spirit of the town and the spirit of the country
2. The spirit of art and the spirit of business
3. The practical spirit and the theoretical spirit
4. Profession and business
5. Farming and agronomy
6. Science and engineering
7. The attitudes of two groups of people on a subject such as gambling, art, money, athletics, or television

FREEMEN AND THOSE WHO ARE NOT FREE *by Edmund Burke*

You will, therefore, not listen to those who tell you that these matters are above you, and ought to be left entirely to those into whose hands the King has put them. The public interest is more

Edmund Burke, *Correspondence of Edmund Burke* (London, 1844).

your business than theirs; and it is from want of spirit, and not from want of ability, that you can become wholly unfit to argue or to judge upon it. For in this very thing lies the difference between freemen and those that are not free. In a free country every man thinks he has a concern in all public matters; that he has a right to form and a right to deliver an opinion upon them. They sift, examine, and discuss them. They are curious, eager, attentive, and jealous; and by making such matters the daily subjects of their thoughts and discoveries, vast numbers contract a very tolerable knowledge of them, and some a very considerable one. And this it is that fills free countries with men of ability in all stations. Whereas in other countries none but men whose office calls them to it having much care or thought about public affairs, and not daring to try the force of their opinions with one another, ability of this sort is extremely rare in any station of life. In free countries, there is often found more real public wisdom and sagacity in shops and manufactories than in the cabinets of princes in countries where none dares to have an opinion until he comes into them. Your whole importance, therefore, depends upon a constant, discreet use of your own reason; otherwise you and your country sink to nothing. If upon any particular occasion you should be roused, you will not know what to do. Your fire will be a fire in straw, fitter to waste and consume yourselves than to warm or enliven anything else. You will be only a giddy mob, upon whom no sort of reliance is to be had. You may disturb your country, but you never can reform your government. . . .

Study Questions

ORGANIZATION AND CONTENT

1. This is a paragraph from a letter written by Edmund Burke, a famous British statesman, on October 13, 1777, to a political club. In order to encourage the members to be concerned with public affairs, Burke contrasts the opportunities and abilities of people in a country like England and those in a country with less freedom. Does he emphasize the positive elements of the contrast or the negative elements?
2. According to sentence 1 the voters of England have what

choice? How is the answer to that question of choice made the basis of the contrast in sentence 3?

3. What is the main point of the sentences devoted to the activities of men in a free country?
4. In which sentences does Burke stress the shortcomings of people in nations without the tradition of freedom?
5. What idea does the *therefore* stand for in sentence 10? What does *otherwise* mean in the second half of sentence 10?
6. In sentences 11–14 Burke predicts things that *will* or *may* happen; they will or may happen if what takes place? On which sentence do all these predictions depend?
7. Sentences 11, 12, and 14 contain contrasts. What are they?
8. Why should Burke mention the idea of "reforming" a government in sentence 14?

SENTENCE STRUCTURE

1. Indicate how emphasis is gained through repetition in sentences 2, 3, and 4.
2. What is the effect of the lists of verbs and adjectives in sentences 5 and 6?
3. Does it seem reasonable that in sentence 9 Burke decided to balance the two different kinds of countries, one at the beginning and the other at the end of the sentence? To what extent does he secure effective emphasis? (Note the problem of handling the four *in*-phrases in sentence 9.)
4. What emphatic contrasts does sentence 9 contain?
5. Explain the principles of organization upon which sentences 11–14 are organized.

DICTION

1. What does "want of spirit" mean (sentence 2)?
2. Explain the precise differences of meaning among the adjectives in sentence 6.
3. Look up *sagacity*, *discreet*.
4. What is the difference between a *factory* and a *manufactory?*

ASSIGNMENT

Write a paragraph contrasting the advantages of one sort of person with the disadvantages of another sort:

1. A lover of reading with one who does not read
2. A nonfraternity member with a fraternity member, or vice versa

3. A college graduate with one who is not a college graduate
4. A person who has traveled with one who has not traveled
5. A person who loves nature with one who does not
6. A person reared in a city with one reared elsewhere

Develop the topic by emphasizing positive aspects and making only occasional reference to the contrasting negative ones. You might do well to assume that your paragraph is from a letter you are writing to a friend encouraging him to do something: for example, travel, attend college, etc.

COMMON LAW AND CIVIL LAW
by Max Radin

1   We began by saying that most civilized communities have a law and could not be without one, since being civilized means being organized, and organization implies a law. But civilization also implies history, and history gives law an individual national character.

2   It is quite true that in western civilized society certain common elements are derived from the common tradition of Christianity and from the institutions of Greece and Rome. Besides these common elements, an entire national system may be borrowed and transplanted into another country, where it inevitably will create a new history of its own and develop in a new way.

3   Within this western civilization, two systems of law have grown up which have in the last century spread beyond their original boundaries. One of these two systems is based on the Roman law. It is misleadingly called the civil law, a term that is used also to describe the noncriminal law of all systems. It has suffered of course extensive changes, and in its modern form is generally found as a code in which the more general ideas of the law are carefully and systematically set forth. Most of these modern codes embodying the civil law are based on the French Civil Code of 1804, and a few on the German Civil Code of 1900 and the Swiss Civil Code of 1907–1911. Nearly all the codes of Latin America are derived from the French.

Max Radin, *The Law and You* (New York, The New American Library of World Literature, 1948). Reprinted by permission of Rhea Radin.

4 The other system is that of the common law of England, which is the basis of the law of England, Ireland, the United States (except Louisiana), all of Canada (except Quebec), Australia, New Zealand, to a less degree India, and to an even lesser degree South Africa. This common law has been codified quite imperfectly in a few American states, but in the main it has remained in the form of a judicial tradition and has not taken statutory form.

5 The civil law and the common law often have been contrasted, and the superiority of one to the other has been made much of by the panegyrist of each. They are much more alike in fundamentals than is generally admitted. The differences are rather matters of detail.

6 One of the most striking differences is in the treatment of property. The common law, in this respect true to its feudal origin, makes a sharp distinction between land and things built on it, or attached to it, and all other kinds of property. The former is called real property or real estate or realty, and the latter, personal property or personalty or sometimes chattels, although personalty and chattels are not quite synonymous. Some kinds of personal rights are associated so definitely with realty that the same rules cover them.

7 Personalty is transferred, leased, hired, mortgaged, lent in very simple ways. As a rule it can be done by word of mouth. It is very different with realty. Most of the transactions in regard to realty must be in writing, and it still is common, although no longer essential, to use exact and elaborate formulas in the deeds, leases, and mortgages by which these transactions are carried out.

8 At the civil law, no such distinction is made, at any rate no such sharp distinction. When property is spoken of, or sales or leases, either kind of property can be meant. But in practice it obviously is impossible to deal with immovables, like land, as though they were exactly like movables. For one thing, the latter can be picked up and literally transferred, and the others cannot. It turns out that differences in legal treatment of movables and immovables, which are very much like personalty and realty, do exist at the civil law although the differences are not so thoroughgoing or extensive.

⁹ The jury system is one of the most famous institutions of the common law. It is used in both civil and criminal cases. Under the Constitution, the right to a trial by jury was declared to be fundamental in both civil and criminal trials. In many of the states, however, a jury may be waived in civil cases and may even be abolished altogether.

¹⁰ The English jury was regarded in England and in Europe generally as a symbol of civic liberty. After the French Revolution, most of the European countries adopted it with modifications but adopted it only for criminal cases. The modifications, however, give the civil law jury a substantially different aspect from that of the common law criminal jury. A majority vote is sufficient for conviction or acquittal. The judges, usually several, vote with the jury. It is usual in the same proceedings—although before the court alone, without a jury—to decide on the money compensation which a convicted criminal must give his victim if such compensation is demanded.

¹¹ On the side of criminal law, there are many differences between the common law and the civil law. Many of the civil rights guaranteed by the Bill of Rights do not exist at the civil law. The right of habeas corpus does not exist there, but we must note that a number of Latin American countries have developed an institution which much resembles it. There is further no right against self-incrimination at the civil law.

¹² But most of the other rules intended to safeguard the rights of an accused exist in both systems. Especially, it may be well to repeat here what was stated before—the common assertion that in the civil law countries there is a presumption of guilt as against the common law presumption of innocence is quite false. The presumption of innocence exists in both systems and, it must be confessed, is not so valuable a safeguard in either as it ought to be.

¹³ If we add to what has been said the fact that, in the modern civil law, statutes are given a much higher place than precedent among sources of law, we have almost exhausted the important differences between the two great modern systems. There are enough indications of mutual adaptation to render it quite possible that, in a federated world, a general law might come into existence which would be a fusion of the two, without destroying

certain special institutions which individual nations may prefer to retain.

Study Questions

ORGANIZATION AND CONTENT

1. What is the function of paragraphs 1 and 2?
2. What does sentence 1 of paragraph 3 lead the reader to expect?
3. To what extent does paragraph 3 satisfy the reader's expectation?
4. What relation does paragraph 4 have to paragraph 3?
5. To what new phase of the subject does paragraph 5 lead the reader?
6. What particular differences between the two systems of law are discussed?
7. How is the material of paragraphs 6–13 proportioned among the subtopics?
8. Make a two-level outline (using Roman numerals and capital letters) of the selection.

SENTENCE STRUCTURE

1. In length and structure do the sentences of this selection most nearly resemble the sentences of the preceding selection by Dobie, by Arnold, or by Burke?
2. To clarify your ideas on this question, analyze the two sentences of paragraph 2 and compare them with sentences 4 and 5 of paragraph 3.
3. Then compare the two sentences of paragraph 4 with the three sentences of paragraph 5.
4. Also compare the sentences of paragraph 10 with those of paragraph 13.

DICTION

1. Look up *codify, statutory, panegyrist, feudal, waive, habeas corpus, presumption, precedent.*
2. Explain the etymology of *realty* and *personalty.*
3. Explain how differences of meaning developed among *chattel, cattle,* and *capital.*
4. Is the diction of this selection more formal or more colloquial than that of the preceding selection by Dobie? By Arnold? By Burke?

Following the same method that Radin used but using a smaller scale, explain similarities and differences between:

1. A junior high school and a senior high school
2. A college and a university
3. A folk song and a ballad
4. Popular music and swing music
5. A Northerner and a Southerner
6. An Easterner and a Westerner
7. Canadians and people of the United States
8. People from two different Latin American or European countries
9. Two Protestant church denominations

UKRAINIANS AND TEXANS
by John Fischer

¹ The Ukrainians are the Texans of Russia. They believe they can fight, drink, ride, sing, and make love better than anybody else in the world, and if pressed will admit it. Their country, too, was a borderland—that's what "Ukraine" means—and like Texas it was originally settled by outlaws, horse thieves, land-hungry farmers, and people who hadn't made a go of it somewhere else. Some of these hard cases banded together, long ago, to raise hell and livestock. They called themselves Cossacks, and they would have felt right at home in any Western movie. Even today the Ukrainians cherish a wistful tradition of horsemanship, although most of them would feel as uncomfortable in a saddle as any Dallas banker. They still like to wear knee-high boots and big, furry hats, made of gray or black Persian lamb, which are the local equivalent of the Stetson.

² Even the country looks a good deal like Texas—flat, dry prairie, shading off in the south to semidesert. Through the middle runs a strip of dark, rich soil, the Chernozom Belt, which is almost identical with the black waxy soil of central Texas. It grows

the best wheat in the Soviet Union. The Ukraine is also famous for its cattle, sheep, and cotton, and—again like Texas—it has been in the throes of an industrial boom for the last twenty years. On all other people the Ukrainians look with a sort of kindly pity. They might have thought up for their own use the old Western rule of etiquette: "Never ask a man where he comes from. If he's a Texan, he'll tell you; if he's not, don't embarrass him."

Study Questions

ORGANIZATION AND CONTENT

1. Can any sentences of the two paragraphs be taken as topic sentences?
2. A comparison might be presented paragraph by paragraph, half-paragraph by half-paragraph, sentence by sentence, and so forth. What is the pattern in which the comparison is presented here?
3. Similarities presented in a comparison might be geographical, historical, traditional, commercial, agricultural, educational, recreational, artistic, psychological, and so forth. What similarities has Fischer stressed in his discussion?
4. Are both parts of the comparison consistently represented?
5. To what extent is suggestion utilized?
6. In which sentences has Fischer referred to specific things or activities in order to make his comparison vivid?

SENTENCE STRUCTURE

1. What transitional links make it easy for the reader to go from sentence to sentence?
2. Just how is the comparison with Texans brought out in sentences 3–7?
3. Fischer's sentences are fairly short. How many are simple, compound, complex?
4. Is the sentence style prevailingly formal or colloquial?

DICTION

1. Look up *wistful, throes.*
2. What is the effect on the reader of using contractions?
3. Is this an example of dignified or undignified writing? Con-

sider phrases like "people who hadn't made a go of it," "hard cases," "to raise hell," "felt right at home."

4. Is it the diction that is responsible for the humorous tone of the selection, or is it something else?

ASSIGNMENT

Most of the selections in this section have shown differences, have developed contrasts; this selection emphasizes likenesses. Imitate it by writing one or two paragraphs showing how two things are alike. Some suggestions:

1. Scientists are like explorers.
2. Successful college life is like disciplined military life.
3. Twentieth-century American painting or architecture or music is like that of other contemporary Western countries.
4. A great man of the present day is like great men of the past.
5. The American of the present is like Americans of the past.
6. Those who live on the sea or in the mountains are like those of the same environment though in different countries.

TWO KINDS OF LITERARY CRITICISM
by Richard G. Moulton

1   It becomes necessary then to recognise two different kinds of literary criticism, as distinct as any two things that can be called by the same name. The difference between the two may be summed up as the difference between the work of a *judge* and of an *investigator*. The one is the enquiry into what ought to be, the other the enquiry into what is. Judicial criticism compares a new production with those already existing in order to determine whether it is inferior to them or surpasses them; criticism of investigation makes the same comparison for the purpose of identifying the new product with some type in the past, or differentiating it and registering a new type. Judicial criticism has a mission to watch against variations from received canons; criticism of investigation watches for new forms to increase its stock of species. The criticism of taste analyses literary works for grounds of

Richard G. Moulton, *Shakespeare as a Dramatic Artist* (Oxford, 1892).

preference or evidence on which to found judgments; inductive criticism analyses them to get a closer acquaintance with their phenomena.

2   Let the question be of Ben Jonson. Judicial criticism starts by holding Ben Jonson responsible for the decay of the English Drama.

3   Inductive criticism takes objection to the word "decay" as suggesting condemnation, but recognises Ben Jonson as the beginner of a new tendency in our dramatic history.

4   But, judicial criticism insists, the object of the Drama is to pourtray human nature, whereas Ben Jonson has painted not men but caricatures.

5   Induction sees that this formula cannot be a sufficient definition of the Drama, for the simple reason that it does not take in Ben Jonson; its own mode of putting the matter is that Ben Jonson has founded a school of treatment of which the law is caricature.

6   But Ben Jonson's caricatures are palpably impossible.

7   Induction soon satisfies itself that their point lies in their impossibility; they constitute a new mode of pourtraying qualities of character, not by resemblance, but by analysing and intensifying contrasts to make them clearer.

8   Judicial criticism can see how the poet was led astray; the bent of his disposition induced him to sacrifice dramatic propriety to his satiric purpose.

9   Induction has another way of putting the matter: that the poet has utilised dramatic form for satiric purpose; thus by the "cross-fertilisation" of two existing literary species he has added to literature a third including features of both.

10   At all events, judicial criticism will maintain, it must be admitted that the Shakespearean mode of pourtraying is infinitely the higher: a signpainter, as Macaulay points out, can imitate a deformity of feature, while it takes a great artist to bring out delicate shades of expression.

11   Inductive treatment knows nothing about higher or lower, which lie outside the domain of science. Its point is that science is indebted to Ben Jonson for a new species; if the new species be an easier form of art, it does not on that account lose its claim to be analysed.

Study Questions

ORGANIZATION AND CONTENT

1. Why should sentence 1 of paragraph 1 be regarded as a topic sentence?
2. What are the key words of contrast in sentence 2?
3. In each half of sentences 3–6 a certain term indicates a kind of critical activity. Identify the words that show the different kinds of activity, and list in two columns the qualities of the different kinds.
4. Ben Jonson is mentioned in paragraph 2. Get more information about Jonson from a history of English literature or a large encyclopedia.
5. To what extent has the author made use of definition in his discussion? How would you explain the way in which the author has employed illustration in his discussion?
6. Paragraphs 2–11 are much shorter than paragraph 1. Why? According to what pattern of thought are paragraphs 2–11 arranged? What are the five points of contrast brought out in paragraphs 2–11?
7. The term *science* is used in paragraph 11. If one type of criticism represents science, what does the other type represent?

SENTENCE STRUCTURE

1. Sentences 3–6 all have two parts; explain the pattern of sentence construction and punctuation by which the parts are balanced in each sentence.
2. To what extent has the principle of contrast influenced sentence structure in paragraphs 2–11?
3. What accounts for the structure of the single sentence of paragraph 6?

DICTION

1. Why does Moulton spell *recognize* and *analyze* with an *s*?
2. Look up *canon, species, taste, inductive, caricature, palpably, induce, portray.*
3. Study and explain the differences between the method of induction and the method of deduction. Is "judicial" criticism based on the method of deduction, or not?

ASSIGNMENT

Imitate Moulton's contrast of the two kinds of criticism by showing:

1. Differences between two styles of playing a game (tennis, baseball, or football)
2. Differences between two methods of housekeeping
3. Differences between two opposing attitudes on the issue of segregation-integration
4. Differences between two political attitudes
5. Differences between cooking by the old-fashioned method with only basic ingredients and the newer "short-cut" method
6. Differences in the ideas and lives of a student much involved in extracurricular activities and a student not involved in them
7. Differences in two cities that have two different types of city government
8. Differences of assumption and feeling in the classical-music enthusiast and the jazz-music enthusiast

In your first paragraph point out in balanced sentences some of the general contrasts involved; then in some shorter paragraphs show particular differences by means of an example.

THE DISTINCTION OF CIVILIZATION AND CULTURE *by Robert M. MacIver*

[1] . . . Let us contrast, say, a factory and a monument, a machine and a picture, a camera and a movie film, a legal document and a play. On the one side we have placed utilitarian objects, means which we employ to satisfy our wants; on the other, things we want, so to speak, for themselves, for the direct satisfaction which they bring us. It is one form of the contrast between means and ends, between the apparatus of living and the expressions of our life. The former we call civilization, the latter culture. By

Robert M. MacIver, *Society: Its Structure and Changes* (Long and Smith, 1931). Revised edition by Robert M. MacIver and Charles H. Page, *Society: An Introductory Analysis*, published by Holt, Rinehart and Winston, Inc. Copyright 1937 by Robert M. MacIver; copyright 1949 by Robert M. MacIver and Charles H. Page.

civilization, then, we mean the whole mechanism and organization which man has devised in his endeavor to control the conditions of his life. It would include not only our systems of social organization but also our techniques and our material instruments. It would include alike the ballot-box and the telephone, the Interstate Commerce Commission and the railroads, our laws as well as our schools, and our banking systems as well as our banks. Culture on the other hand is the expression of our nature in our modes of living and of thinking, in our everyday intercourse, in art, in literature, in religion, in recreation and enjoyment. While, as we shall see, many objects possess both a civilizational and a cultural element, we can often decide the question of their classification by asking: do we want these things themselves or do we merely use them in order to attain some other thing we want? Do they exist because of some outer necessity or because we seek them as such? Often we make a virtue of necessity and impress on utilitarian objects a cultural quality, as when we build banks to rival temples, but if these objects would not exist at all for the *direct* satisfaction they yield us we may classify them as within the category of civilization. On the other hand many objects combine both elements so inextricably, for example our clothing and our homes, that we must be content simply to distinguish the two aspects of the service they render.

2   The distinction between the two categories is seen in the way they respectively enter into the social heritage. An achievement of civilization is generally exploited and improved, going on from strength to strength, until it is superseded or rendered obsolete by some new invention. It is true that in past ages some achievements of civilization have again been lost. Men forgot the arts which raised the pyramids of Egypt and which constructed the roads and aqueducts of the Romans. But these losses occurred through catastrophic changes which blotted out the records of civilization. With the widening of the areas of civilization and with superior methods of recording discoveries any utilitarian or technical gain becomes a permanent possession within the social heritage and the condition of further gains. Civilization is thus a cumulative process, a "march." It is otherwise with cultural achievements. They do not lead assuredly to higher or improved ones. Since man first invented the automobile, it has continuously

improved. Our means of transportation grow constantly more swift and more efficient. They are vastly superior to those which the ancient Greeks employed. But can we say the same of our dramas and our sculptures, our conversation and our recreation? Here certitude fails us. There are no automobiles to-day so comparatively inefficient as the first vehicles of Henry Ford—his work and that of other inventors inevitably prepared the way for better ones. But our plays are not necessarily better to-day because of the achievements of Shakespeare. There is no "march" of culture. It is subject to retrogression as well as to advance. Its past does not assure its future.

3   In a word, the social heritage does not ensure the future of culture with the same probability with which it provides the conditions of civilization. Culture, being the immediate expression of the human spirit, can advance only if that spirit is capable of finer efforts, has itself something more to express. Civilization is the vehicle of culture: its improvement is no guarantee of finer quality in that which it conveys. The radio can carry our words to the ends of the earth, but the words need be no wiser on that account. The civilization around us can be enjoyed without any special effort, without any particular merit on our part. The culture we "inherit" is ours only if we are worthy of it. A new generation cannot enjoy the culture of the past unless they win it afresh for themselves. Culture is communicated only to the like-minded. No one without the quality of the artist can appreciate art, nor without the ear of the musician can one enjoy music. Civilization in general makes no such demand. We can enjoy its products without sharing the capacity which creates them. Moreover, the process of creation itself is different. Lesser minds improve the work of the great inventors, but lesser poets do not improve on Shakespeare. The product of the artist is more revelatory of his personality than is that of the technician, just as the quality of a people is peculiarly expressed in its culture rather than in its civilization.

4   This more intimate relation of culture and society is seen also in the fact that culture is not transferable in the simple mode characteristic of civilization. Given adequate means of communication, any improvement in the apparatus of life will quickly spread. In fact with the modern development of communications

a single system of civilization is already encompassing nearly all the earth. Even the savage is ready to discard his bow and spear and to adopt the rifle. The power-machine displaces the hand tool wherever men have the means to acquire it. The corporate form of industry encroaches everywhere on older forms as irresistibly as the factory displaces the domestic system of production. We have pointed out that these techniques are readily comparable and the relative superiority of one over the other is easily adjudged. Civilization has its objective tests so that it is a simple matter to decide that one mode of hygiene or one method of road-building is preferable to another. The advance of civilization is seriously resisted only when the older form is closely associated with the culture of a people. For a people will not freely abandon its culture for another, since to do so would be to sacrifice its intrinsic quality. Even when one civilization covers the globe great cultural differences, modified as they become under such conditions, will endure, just as they endure to-day among the industrialized peoples. It is true that cultural "borrowing" occurs, but it is selective and seemingly wayward, dependent on a degree of affinity, of like-mindedness, in the borrowers and always colored or even distorted by their personality. The history of religious conversion and proselytism affords sufficient evidences of this selective process. The Geneva of Calvin and the Scotland of Knox and the Massachusetts of Cotton Mather were receptive of certain strains in the multiform tradition of Christianity, selecting ascetic, authoritarian, patriarchal, eschatological elements within it and translating them into a system which they identified with Christianity itself, just as other peoples and other times selected and transmuted other elements to form their creeds. It may also be noted that this selective "borrowing" is not limited to recent or contemporaneous contributions to the stock of culture. In this also it differs from the process by which civilization spreads. Culture elements may be adopted as readily from the past as from the present, from any epoch of the past no less than from the present hour. Cultural affinity may revert to the legends of Greece or of the German forests, to the art of tenth-century China or of pre-Raphaelite Florence, to the meditations of Job or of Marcus Aurelius. Its range of selection runs from the newest culture-fashion to the myths that linger from the dawn of history.

⁵ In the light of these distinctions it is obvious that the expansion of a civilization follows different principles from those which determine cultural development. Where communications admit, the former tends to proceed more rapidly, more simply, less selectively, always spreading outwards from the foci of technological and economic advance. The products of civilization are conveyed over every trade route, and they prepare the way for the techniques and systems which created them. People trade with one another before they understand one another. The expansion of civilization has perils on that very account. For the interdependence of peoples within a common civilization outstrips the formation of those cultural attitudes necessary for its maintenance. This peril was glaringly exposed in the Great War. The spread of civilization makes certain cultural readjustments imperative.

Study Questions

ORGANIZATION AND CONTENT

1. Explain the movement from the specific to the general which takes place in sentences 1–4.
2. What relation have sentences 5–7 with sentences 8–11?
3. Is there any reason why sentence 12 should be the last sentence of paragraph 1?
4. Can you identify topic sentences in paragraphs 2–5?
5. How does paragraph 3 differ in emphasis from paragraph 2?
6. What do "objective tests" of civilization have to do with the "simple mode" of its transfer? What term relating to culture contrasts with "objective tests"?
7. What further differences between civilization and culture are pointed out in the latter part of paragraph 4?
8. What is the most important idea of paragraph 5?
9. How many specific examples does MacIver use in each paragraph? Is there any reason why there should be more of them in one paragraph than another?
10. Which examples are the most effective? the least easy to understand?
11. Contrasts may be organized paragraph by paragraph, sentence by sentence, and so on. What method of organizing the contrast has MacIver employed? Has he been systematic? In this

respect does the selection by MacIver most resemble, or most differ from, the selection by Moulton, Radin, Arnold, or Dobie?

12. This contrast contains elements of analysis and definition. Does the discussion of civilization and culture by a famous sociologist have any agreement with the definitions by Churchill (statesman), Bell (art critic), and Brodrick (anthropologist)?

SENTENCE STRUCTURE

1. By what sentence patterns has the author indicated contrasts in paragraph 1? Point out different specific patterns.
2. Indicate special terms and phrases used for transition in the contrasts of paragraphs 1–3.
3. Does the author use any different type of sentence for his examples from that which he uses in the rest?
4. One might expect that contrasts would be brought out especially by compound sentences. Has MacIver used a large proportion of compound sentences?
5. Has he used other patterns of grammatical parallelism?
6. Which paragraph contains the shortest sentences? Do they have an effect of choppiness, forceful emphasis, crisp summary, or what?

DICTION

1. Look up *inextricably, heritage, exploited, peculiarly, encroaches, intrinsic, proselytism, ascetic, eschatological, pre-Raphaelite, imperative.*
2. From what language do the following words come? *utilitarian, supersede, aqueduct, retrogression, encompass, patriarchal, foci.* Learn the meanings of the roots as well as of the words.
3. How significant is MacIver's use of metaphor—for example, his calling civilization *apparatus* and *mechanism?*
4. What implications are suggested by other metaphors: the "march" of civilization, and civilization as the "vehicle" of culture?
5. Is the term "social heritage" a metaphor or not?

ASSIGNMENT

Write one or two substantial paragraphs in which you:

1. Contrast the state of civilization and culture in your home town

2. Contrast an artist and a technician
3. Either contrast or compare a temple and a modern bank
4. Bring out the differing qualities of peoples with contrasting cultures
5. Show the differences between persons who "win culture afresh for themselves" and those who simply take advantage of the civilization about them "without any special effort"

(Elsewhere MacIver has written of the inventions of American civilization as "foolproof," that is, able to be used without effort by people who are completely ignorant of how they operate.)

III Argument

AN ARGUMENT
is not a quarrel. Originally to argue meant to make clear, and thus
to show, to prove, to give evidence. An argument is a presenting
of reasons for or reasons against something; it implies that the person who states an argument has tried to understand the matter
in question and that he is using his powers of reason to show why
evidence supports his position. The setting forth of a conviction
or belief and the evidence for it does not need to imply any
opposition. Perhaps everyone in the world would agree with the
argument.

However, there is always potential disagreement with an
argument; and on many matters people disagree. An argument
for one side of a question calls forth an opposing argument from
a person who disagrees. When two people engage in argument,
they disagree. When two people quarrel, they also disagree. But
a quarrel implies that they become angry; they may call each
other names, make threats, shake their fists, break off friendly
relations. When they are so filled with emotion, they are not
likely to be very reasonable. It is hard to think of either person
winning a quarrel.

In an argument, however, one person may win. If he wins,
he wins because his *evidence* is greater in quantity or superior in
importance to the evidence of the other person, or because he
reasons better, shows more clearly the logical conclusions that
must be drawn from the material. Even the opponent may be
completely convinced by the winning argument—particularly if
he has not thought very much or very deeply about the subject
before. To win an argument properly, then, one should have

both knowledge that provides evidence and good powers of reasoning. To become violently emotional, to become quarrelsome, unpleasant, or nasty, is not likely to help one to argue well.

Many people, when they find that someone else disagrees with them, tend to start a quarrel rather than an argument. They may make attacks on the other person's character, accuse him of selfish motives for his beliefs, treat his reasoning and evidence with scoffing and sarcasm. They may be tempted to repeat, more and more loudly, the thing that they believe. Then they may become exasperated when asked to give reasons for their belief. The apprentice writer is likely to need practice, therefore, in argument, so that he will not confuse an argument with a quarrel or mistake sarcasm for evidence.

The next step for the apprentice writer is to learn (it seems to be difficult for many people) that mere assertion has no value in argument. There are any number of assertions which people make, and their statements may represent very strong belief, yet such statements, without evidence, will not convince another person that they are true. People disagree on a great many questions, but often they disagree because they have not thought enough about these questions, because they have not gathered evidence or have not analyzed the evidence to discover what it really means.

Below are some examples of assertions that are often made (but other people may disagree and therefore argue):

> The team is better this year than last.
> This novel is well written (or dramatic, significant, etc.).
> Everyone should vote for Candidate X.
> Smoke PQR cigars for the best flavor.
> President X was right (or wrong).
> Senator X was wrong (or right).
> Take this course, not that one.
> Mr. ABC is a better teacher (singer, scientist, etc.) than XYZ.

Many assertions will immediately bring exactly opposite statements of belief from some listener or reader. For example:

> We should raise taxes—tax property owners more.
> We should lower taxes—exempt the property owners.

> We ought to have censorship of "comic" books.
> No, we ought to have complete freedom of the press.

We ought to take Latin (a dead language) out of the curriculum!

No, we ought to make *everybody* study Latin!

Children need more discipline!

No, more freedom!

Such assertions immediately raise questions in the minds of those who hear them. Listeners will say: "You have made a statement, you two have made opposing statements. But what *is* the truth of the matter? What *should* we do? What course *should* we follow?" In order to answer these questions, of course, evidence must be produced. "What is the truth?" is a question of fact. Often it can be satisfactorily answered, sometimes easily answered. If it is asserted that Mrs. A's living room is longer than Mrs. B's, the truth can be found just by taking a tape measure or a yardstick and measuring the two rooms. In such a situation there could properly be no argument. Often questions can be settled (and quarrels avoided) by the simple means of looking up the facts.

However, very frequently the facts are not so easily found; and sometimes, even when found, they do not automatically decide an argument. Suppose someone says, "Team X is better than Team Y." If arrangements could be made for the two teams to play several games, then very likely the evidence would be clear; people would say that the question of fact had been answered. If such arrangements could not be made, many facts about the teams, all sorts of records, may be listed; yet whether the assertion is true or not may still be a matter of doubt. Of course, the question of fact involved in the assertion "Our team this year is better than our team was last year" cannot be settled by playing. It is impossible for the two teams in question to play any games. It would be necessary to work on the question of fact entirely by statistics. Similarly, two teams of the same year may not have a chance to play against each other enough to show without doubt which is the better team, so that it is then necessary to gather statistical evidence to try to settle the question of fact. This sort of evidence will never be so convincing as the scores of actual games.

Without clear evidence of actual scores, the question of whether one team is "better" than the other cannot be measured like two living rooms; it is not a simple question of fact alone. Interpretation of facts is involved; and evaluation may enter in. Many people will be inclined to "weight" or "discount" some of the evidence. Will it not make a difference whether a team is excellent in defensive strength, or capacity to take advantage of opponents' mistakes, or speed, or deceptiveness, or plodding power?

Yet questions of fact and questions of fact-plus-interpretation are usually easier to deal with than questions of policy, questions in which *should* is the key word. "Everybody should study Latin. Children should have more freedom. The United States should enter the European Common Market." Such propositions involve judgment as well as fact; they involve the weighing of facts; they involve values; and they may involve experience as well as information. Judgments are based upon standards that people accept; that is, they are based upon certain assumptions regarding what is valuable. And when one is trying to look into the future (which one must always do when a question of policy is being argued), his argument may depend strongly upon his reasoning from what has happened in the past—and this is why the light that experience gives may play an important part in deciding arguments on questions of policy.

At any rate, in all arguments the evidence should have a bearing upon the question (it must be *relevant*), it should be presented *logically*, and it should have the power to convince (it should be *cogent*).

Here is an example of argument from ancient Greece. The men of Corcyra and the men of Corinth went to war over the city of Epidamnum, and those of Corcyra won. Then for two years the Corinthians built up their navy, and the men of Corcyra became alarmed. They decided in 433 B.C. that they would join the Athenian alliance and get help from Athens, if they could, against Corinth. According to the Greek historian Thucydides they presented their argument to the men of Athens as follows:

> Those who, like ourselves, come to others who are not their allies and to whom they have never rendered any considerable service and ask help of them, are bound to show, in the first place, that the granting of their request is expedient, or at any rate not inexpedient, and, secondly, that their gratitude will be lasting. If

they fulfil neither requirement they have no right to complain of a refusal. . . .

To you at this moment the request which we are making offers a glorious opportunity. In the first place, you will assist the oppressed and not the oppressors; secondly, you will admit us to your alliance at a time when our vital interests are at stake, and will lay up a treasure of gratitude in our memories which will have the most abiding of all records. Lastly, we have a navy greater than any but your own. Reflect; what good fortune can be more extraordinary, what more annoying to your enemies than the voluntary accession of a power for whose alliance you would have given any amount of money and could never have been too thankful. This power now places herself at your disposal.

In formal terms, the argument of the men of Corcyra is on the *proposition*, Athens *should* take Corcyra into alliance and give it help. They are bound to show, they say, two things, in order to convince the Athenians: (1) that granting the request is expedient; (2) that Corcyra will feel lasting gratitude.

These two things are the points upon which argument will center. They are the *issues* of the argument. It is important in an efficient argument that both the proposition and the issues be clearly brought out.

What evidence do the representatives of Corcyra use to support their side of the argument? Their first assertion is intended to support the issue of gratitude; it depends for effectiveness on the idea that those who are being oppressed will feel more gratitude for assistance than will the oppressors; their second assertion that Corcyra will feel gratitude rests on the idea that those who receive help when their vital interests are at stake will be especially grateful for assistance. It implies a sequence of reasoning—a syllogism of *deductive logic*. The syllogism is:

Major Premise: Those who are in great danger are very grateful for help.

Minor Premise: Corcyra is in great danger from Corinth.

Conclusion: Therefore Corcyra will be very grateful for help from Athens.

If a syllogism is true, the premises must be true. If a person believes in the truth of the major premise of this syllogism, he must have made an evaluation based on his judgment of human nature or upon cases that he has learned about from the past which support this interpretation of human nature. If one believes in the major premise because of cases observed in the past, he has used *inductive logic.* The process is as follows: (1) In Case A help was given in time of danger and gratitude was shown. (2) In Case B the same thing happened. (3) In Case C the same thing happened. . . . If there is a sufficiently large number of cases in which the same result is observed, then it will be thought that the probability is very high that the same result will always occur. Not a certainty but a probability. That is, if the series of cases were indefinitely extended, one would expect to learn that in Case N gratitude would also be shown. But the cases cannot actually be extended indefinitely. Therefore, one must make what is called an *inductive leap* to the conclusion; one must leap over all the other cases which may exist but which have not been examined, on to Case N representing the last in the possible series, expecting that on the basis of the cases already observed, the same thing will hold true. Thus the truth of the major premise would be arrived at: *All* who are in great danger are grateful for help.

If there were any exceptions among the cases examined, the probability of the inductive conclusion would, of course, be weakened. This idea is brought out in the old saying that "the exception proves the rule," which does not mean that an exception gives a proof of the rule but that an exception tests the rule, that is, the conclusion or generalization. If an example were found in which people were not grateful for help even when in great danger, the conclusion would have to be modified to something like "Nearly all people are grateful. . . ." or "All people except Persians are grateful. . . ."

At any rate inductive logic and deductive logic go together and support each other. For example, it must have taken a good many observations to establish the rule that at sea level water freezes at 32 degrees Fahrenheit. But once this inductive conclusion had been established, it could be used to cover every individual case of water when the temperature was likely to go down to 32 degrees. In such a case one would know that to keep water from freezing he must plan to use antifreeze, make a fire, add hot water, or take some such measure. Such a universal proposition, well based in induction, gives the human mind an enormous amount of practical power.

The second issue of the argument by the men of Corcyra is supported by their pointing out to the Athenians that it would be expedient for Athens to add the strength of another large navy to that of the Athenian navy. Such a statement about national military forces would doubtless be regarded as self-evident. But it, too, rests upon conclusions of inductive logic and also an implied deductive syllogism. The student will not find it difficult to establish the logical bases of this part of the argument. Certainly in all that they say the men of Corcyra intend to convince the Athenians that to give them help would be completely reasonable.

Yet there are two modifications of the preceding ideas that should be kept in mind. In the first place, though it is bad to become overemotional to the point that reason, evidence, and logic are tossed aside, an argument does not have to be utterly cold and unemotional. Naturally, personal feeling enters into much argument, both spoken and written. And the presence of such feeling may help very much to make the argument seem convincing. A good example of personal feeling helping the effectiveness of an argument is the famous funeral oration of Marc Antony for Julius Caesar in Shakespeare's *Julius Caesar*. Brutus had spoken briefly and rather coldly: he said that he honored Caesar for many good qualities—"but, as he was ambitious, I slew him." (*Ambitious* here means aggressively determined to seize power.) Marc Antony's speech is, in terms of argument, largely a refutation of the idea that Caesar was "ambitious." He cites several pieces of evidence indicating that Caesar was not, after all, really "ambitious."

> He was my friend, faithful and just to me:
> But Brutus says he was ambitious;
> And Brutus is an honourable man.
> He hath brought many captives home to Rome,
> Whose ransoms did the general coffers fill:
> Did this in Caesar seem ambitious?
> When that the poor have cried, Caesar hath wept:
> Ambition should be made of sterner stuff:

Yet Brutus says he was ambitious;
And Brutus is an honourable man.
You all did see that on the Lupercal
I thrice presented him a kingly crown,
Which he did thrice refuse: was this ambition?
Yet Brutus says he was ambitious;
And sure he is an honourable man.
I speak not to disprove what Brutus spoke,
But here I am to speak what I do know.

Since Antony had been ordered by Brutus to say nothing against the conspirators who had killed Caesar, Antony kept the letter of the order; but he was trying to persuade the crowd that the conspirators were really murderers—"butchers"—and not saviors of Rome. So Antony mentions four pieces of evidence: faithful friendship, captives, sympathy with the poor, refusal of a crown, all of which contradict the idea of ruthless, aggressive "ambition." Furthermore, he uses two questions—"rhetorical" questions—which provide a personal contact with the audience, and he mentions himself and his own feeling—note the emphasis of "just to *me*" and "here I am to speak what *I do know*." Such sincerely felt emotion will impress the audience. But Antony does not allow the emotion to get out of control; he systematically cites four examples intended to refute the veracity of the motives Brutus had alleged. We should say, then, that although over-emotional arguments are not good, emotion in argument is not ruled out. Some authorities give the name of persuasion to arguments that have emotional appeals.

In the second place, though arguments should be logical, considerable use is made in argument of analogy, and analogy does not force one to inescapable logical conclusions. Nevertheless, similarities between situations, when such similarities exist, cause people to tend to think that the situation being argued about should be treated in the same manner that a former situation was treated. The effect of analogy may be expressed in such a phrase as "the same treatment for the same disease"; or it may be regarded as a kind of extension of the mathematical axiom that things equal to the same thing are equal to each other.

John Locke, a seventeenth-century philosopher, believed that a young man should not be kept without any knowledge of worldly matters, even though there is evil in the world. Locke argued that it was especially important to have a tutor teach a knowledge of "men and their manners." The pupil should be "warned who are like to oppose, who to mislead, who to undermine him, and who to serve him. He should be instructed how to know and distinguish them."

Locke then uses an analogy in his argument.

Therefore I think it of most value to be instilled into a young man upon all occasions which offer themselves that when he comes to launch into the deep himself he may not be like one at sea without a line, compass or sea-chart, but may have some notice beforehand of the rocks and shoals, the currents and quicksands, and know a little how to steer that he sink not before he get experience.

In Locke's analogy the world is like the ocean, and the young man is like a captain who has the responsibility of sailing a ship safely through the ocean. The dangers and evils of the world are like rocks, shoals, and quicksand. Knowledge of the world gained from a tutor is like a compass and a chart, which supply information regarding the ocean.

If it seems reasonable that a captain should have experience and knowledge of the ocean, then it should seem reasonable that a young man should have knowledge and experience of the world. Locke was certainly assuming that the likenesses between the two situations were significant ones. Unless they were, his analogy would be worthless. And though likenesses may exist, the analogy does not *prove* the point. Possibly worldly knowledge might damage the character of the young man in a way that knowledge of the sea would not harm the capabilities of a captain for handling a ship. One situation in the analogy concerns a physical matter or problem; but the other situation concerns a moral and psychological problem. Therefore, this analogy, and all analogies, must be viewed with some caution. They may be very effective illustrations, but they are not proofs.

Locke made the assumption that knowledge of evils is a significant requirement for success in managing one's life, just as knowledge of the location of rocks and quicksands is a significant requirement for success in sailing a ship. Yet he did not state clearly that he was making that assumption. Assumptions are often hidden in arguments. They are often taken for granted—that is, the speaker feels that the assumption he makes is so reasonable, so natural, so unquestionable, that he does not even realize that other people may regard it differently. Consequently, it is essential to be on guard for this tendency in all arguments; one ought to test his own arguments as well as those of opponents to find out what assumptions have actually been made.

In a sense, of course, all exposition is argument; that is, the writer wishes the reader to feel satisfied that what he has written is true. It was stated earlier that each paragraph should contain evidence to support the topic idea. The writer wants the reader to say to himself, "Yes, this paragraph is a solid one; I believe what the writer says"—perhaps that two things are similar, or that the meaning of a term has changed, or that a machine has four main sections, or that a certain man was both brilliant and responsible. . . . But, in the kind of writing properly called argument, the writer is presenting a *justification* of his belief, his opinion, his judgment, his preference; he is always trying to convince the reader that he is *right* and frequently he is trying to persuade the reader that the reader ought to do something: cast a ballot, purchase an article, give money, write a letter, use his influence. . . . And this is why arguers are tempted to use tricks—anything to get the reader to do the thing desired.

Honorable people ought not, however, to try to trick other people in argument. To use devices of "one-upmanship" or to use fallacies in argument is improper. *Fallacies* are falsities of argument—tricky, deceptive, *faulty* ways of persuasion. There are many of them. A recent book[1] lists 51 fallacies classified under "Material Fallacies," such as faulty generalization and faulty analogy; "Psychological Fallacies," such as abusing the emotional power of words, ridicule, or appealing to prejudice; and "Logical Fallacies," such as the undistributed middle term in a syllogism, circular definition, and begging the question. If the apprentice writer has the opportunity to take a course in logic or in argumentation, he will become more skillful in detecting fallacies. But, in the meantime, he as an apprentice writer can consistently try to be fair and logical in all his arguments.

[1] W. Ward Fearnside and William B. Holther, *Fallacy: The Counterfeit of Argument* (Englewood Cliffs, N.J., Prentice-Hall, Inc., 1959).

In writing arguments, one will, of course, make use of all of the other forms of writing that have been set forth in this text. Definitions appear in arguments—in fact, defining terms is often necessary so that people can agree on exactly what the argument is about—as do analysis, enumeration, comparison and contrast; all of these types of writing have their function. There may even be examples of description, characterization, and narrative, as writers undertake to make people understand historical backgrounds, physical situations, and the attitudes of people involved in public questions.

The Committee for Cultural Freedom, which was established in 1939, set forth a Code of Ethics to be followed in political controversy. Mr. Sidney Hook was the main author of this Code.

These are the ten points by which we think all political controversy ought to be guided:

1. Nothing and no one is immune from criticism.
2. Everyone involved in a controversy has an intellectual responsibility to inform himself of the available facts.
3. Criticism should be directed first to policies and against persons only when they are responsible for policies, and against their motives or purposes only when there is some independent evidence of their character.
4. Because certain words are legally permissible, they are not therefore morally permissible.
5. Before impugning an opponent's motives, even when they legitimately may be impugned, answer his arguments.
6. Do not treat an opponent of a policy as if he were therefore a personal enemy, or an enemy of the country, or a concealed enemy of democracy.
7. Since a good cause may be defended by bad arguments, after answering the bad arguments for another's position, present positive evidence for your own.
8. Do not hesitate to admit lack of knowledge or to suspend judgment if evidence is not decisive either way.
9. Because something is logically possible, it is not therefore probable. "It is not impossible" is a preface to an irrelevant statement about human affairs. The question is always one of the balance of probabilities.
10. The cardinal sin, when we are looking for truth of fact or wisdom of policy, is refusal to discuss, or action which blocks discussion.

These are wise rules to observe in all arguments. They apply especially to politics, but whether one is trying to convince scientists that something they had not known before is really true (like William Harvey presenting the case for the circulation of the blood), whether one is arguing for a particular business policy or defending a client in a law case or showing why a college curriculum needs changes or why art enriches life or why a Beethoven symphony has higher esthetic value than a popular song—no matter what the area of argument, one does best to argue honestly, with pertinent evidence, good reasoning, and good manners.

The readings that follow can be divided into two general groups. The first group—from Commager through Russell—could be conveniently classified as examples of Evidence for Proof; the second group—those from Emerson through Mumford—as More Complex Arguments.

CARELESSNESS IS EVIDENT THROUGHOUT AMERICAN LIFE
by Henry Steele Commager

1   Carelessness was perhaps the most pervasive and persistent quality in the American. He was careless about himself, his speech, his dress, his food, even his manners; those who did not know him thought him slovenly and rude. His attitude toward the English language pained the traditionalists, but he brought to language and grammar something of the same vitality and ingenuity that he brought to his work or his religion, and they served his needs and reflected his character. He was careless about rank and class, about tradition and precedent, about the rights and prerogatives of others and about his own rights and prerogatives. He tolerated in others minor infractions of law or custom and expected to be similarly indulged in his own transgressions: hence his vast patience with noise, litter, the invasion of privacy, and

Henry Steele Commager, *The American Mind* (New Haven, Yale University Press, 1950).

sharp practices. Although he had, as it were, invented time, he did not, like his English cousins, make a fetish of punctuality, nor did he celebrate the hours with such ritual as tea or dressing for dinner. He was careless about his work and his trade, and, preferring to have machines work for him, he regarded with equanimity the decline of inherited traditions of craftsmanship. While the products of his machines could compete anywhere in the world market, the products of his handicraft could not.

2   The American took, in fact, little pride in a finished job, prizing versatility above thoroughness. He was the world's most successful farmer, but his cultivation was gargantuan rather than intensive, and scientific agriculture lagged a generation or more behind that of Europe while, after the eighteenth century, landscape gardening was regarded as a European rather than an American art. The construction of the transcontinentals was one of the greatest engineering feats of modern history, but the American's railway tracks, like his roads, had to be rebuilt every few years. Every town and city confessed the same characteristic —whole sections only half built, houses falling down a decade after they had been put up, ambitious plans unfulfilled. A ragged, unfinished quality characterized much of his culture. He undertook the most gigantic educational program in history, but it was the universal opinion that American education was eclectic rather than thorough. His speech revealed his impatience: he slurred over his words, left his sentences unfinished, and developed to the full the possibilities of slang. Neither transcendentalism nor pragmatism, the two ways of thinking that can properly be designated American, had a systematic quality, and it was suggestive that his most characteristic form of philosophy, pragmatism, should emphasize the unfinished nature of the universe. Many Americans preferred their preachers untrained, and most of them distrusted the professional soldier.

Study Questions

ORGANIZATION AND CONTENT

1. Do these two paragraphs have topic sentences? If so, what are they?
2. What is the nature of the evidence Commager uses to convince the reader that Americans are careless?

3. Is there enough evidence to convince his audience?
4. In what different areas of life is American carelessness revealed?
5. Does it matter which pieces of Commager's evidence are presented first or presented last?
6. Sentence 5 of paragraph 2 is a general statement. What justifies such a general statement at this point?
7. Is Commager willing to grant that American life has anything noteworthy to compensate for carelessness?
8. Is there any reason why a philosophy of pragmatism should be developed in a culture which carelessness pervades?

SENTENCE STRUCTURE

1. Indicate transitional links among the author's sentences.
2. What is the effect of repetition of grammatical patterns here: for instance, "He was careless about"?
3. Indicate parallelism of structure in sentences 2–5.
4. In which sentences of both paragraphs does Commager bring out contrasts? By what means?
5. To what extent do the sentences have variety in the way they begin?
6. Do these sentences have too much similarity of pattern: too many *and*'s, for example?

DICTION

1. Look up *pervasive, ingenuity, precedent, infractions, transgressions, versatility*. What other words are based on the same roots as these?
2. Look up *prerogatives, fetish, ritual, equanimity, eclectic, slang, transcendentalism, pragmatism*.
3. What accounts for the form and meaning of *gargantuan?*

ASSIGNMENT

Give a considerable amount of evidence to convince someone that a certain condition exists. For example:

1. _____ is the most pervasive quality of students at this college.
2. Generosity is a persistent quality in American life.
3. Americans tend to be suspicious of foreigners.
4. The life of people in North America is a wholesome one.
5. Americans are an extravagant people.

WHY CONVERSATION IS VALUABLE
by Michel de Montaigne

The most fruitful and natural exercise of the mind, in my opinion, is conversation; I find the use of it more sweet than of any other action of life; and for that reason it is that, if I were now compelled to choose, I should sooner, I think, consent to lose my sight, than my hearing and speech. The Athenians, and also the Romans, kept this exercise in great honour in their academies; the Italians retain some traces of it to this day, to their great advantage, as is manifest by the comparison of our understandings with theirs. The study of books is a languishing and feeble motion that heats not, whereas conversation teaches and exercises at once. If I converse with an understanding man, and a rough disputant, he presses hard upon me, and pricks me on both sides; his imaginations raise up mine to more than ordinary pitch; jealousy, glory, and contention, stimulate and raise me up to something above myself; and concurrence is a quality totally offensive in discourse. But, as our minds fortify themselves by the communication of vigorous and regular understandings, 'tis not to be expressed how much they lose and degenerate by the continual commerce and frequentation we have with such as are mean and weak; there is no contagion that spreads like that; I know sufficiently by experience what 'tis worth a yard. I love to discourse and dispute, but it is with but few men, and for myself; for to do it as a spectacle and entertainment to great persons, and to make of a man's wit and words competitive parade, is, in my opinion, very unbecoming a man of honour.

Study Questions

ORGANIZATION AND CONTENT

1. Montaigne says that *in his opinion* conversation is "the most fruitful and natural exercise of the mind." If this idea is to be thought something more than a whim, what should Montaigne (or any person expressing an opinion) be prepared to do?

Michel de Montaigne, *The Essays of Michel de Montaigne*, trans. by Charles Cotton, ed. with notes by W. Carew Hazlitt (1892).

2. What historical support does he give this opinion? Does Montaigne do well to mention this point where he does, or would it be more effective somewhere else?
3. What other reasons besides historical ones does Montaigne present to justify his opinion?
4. What does sentence 4 contribute to the discussion?
5. Sentence 4 is placed close to the middle of the paragraph. Why is this sentence of particular importance in the paragraph?
6. At what points in the paragraph does Montaigne bring in negative contrasts?
7. How might sentence 6 be regarded as answering a possible objection?

SENTENCE STRUCTURE

1. Sentence 1 is divided into three parts: explain why part two follows part one and part three follows part two.
2. What dramatic effect does sentence 1 have?
3. Why does the structure of sentence 2 call for a semicolon?
4. What are the two contrasted terms in sentence 3?
5. Sentence 5 contains the words *minds fortify themselves;* what terms in sentence 4 do these words parallel?
6. What opposite idea does *but* introduce in sentence 5?

DICTION

1. Can you justify the adjectives *fruitful* and *natural* in sentence 1?
2. Look up *academies, pitch, glory, contention, stimulate, fortify, commerce, concurrence* (why spelled with two *r*'s?).
3. Which of these words have Latin roots?

ASSIGNMENT

Select some experience which *in your opinion* is especially enjoyable, valuable, or useful; then explain what reasons you have for holding this opinion: that is, for believing that your judgment about this matter is *true.* Possibilities are:

1. Reading one book each week
2. Remaining entirely alone for one afternoon each week
3. Taking part in a community enterprise
4. Developing proficiency in some sport or athletic or musical activity
5. Reading Shakespeare, Chaucer, Dickens, Mark Twain, Emerson, or some other author

6. Learning to cook
7. Furnishing a room according to one's own taste
8. Traveling
9. Living in a large city
10. Living close to the sea

Follow the model closely. In the first sentence explain the main idea and state why you would rather have this experience than some other. Give a historical example to support your opinion. Contrast the experience you are arguing for with some other that is less enjoyable or valuable.

WHY THE AMERICAN MIDWEST MAY BECOME THE SEAT OF A CIVILIZATION ON A GRAND SCALE
by *Alfred North Whitehead and Lucien Price*

1   "In the Midwest, climate, soil, and food—those three preconditions to a flourishing civilization — are favourable. Man's earliest essays in recorded civilizations occur in hot climates where food is abundant and clothes and shelter next to needless. Rice, in large part, sustained the civilization of India; in Mesopotamia a civilized society arose on grain; in Egypt the food staple was mainly the date; in Central and South America among the Aztecs and Incas it was maize and the banana. But over-population, made possible by cheap food, cheapens labour and opens the way to political despotism; and although the wealth, and hence the leisure requisite for culture may result from cheap labour, the consequent loss of liberty stultifies the intellect. Thus it was that in Europe, a colder climate, where food, clothes, and shelter are harder to get, and where proliferation of the human species is not so exuberant but individuality is more pronounced, our northern civilization ventured into rational thought, thought less shackled by religious superstition, and finally produced that energetic and self-reliant creature, European man."

2 "Nearly every variety of European man is somewhere in our Midwest."

3 "It has a human soil further favourable to a new civilization: not only is it a self-selected stock; the country people and the people in small towns still hold a favourably large proportion as compared with the population of cities. Man's best thinking is done either by persons living in the country or in small communities, or else by those who, having had such environment in early life, enrich their experience by life in cities; for what is wanted is contact with the elemental processes of nature during those years of youth when the mind is being formed."

4 "How often have I noticed that as between country boys or boys from small towns, and city boys or boys brought up in the suburbs," I said, "how much more self-reliant and resourceful the country-bred lads are. Suppose they lose their jobs: the city or suburban boy, who is usually from the white-collar class, is generally upset and feels rather helpless; your country boy will be cool as a cucumber. What of it? He has earned his living by working with his hands, and he could do it again if necessary."

5 "Urbanization," Whitehead continued, "is a weakness in much of our modern thinking, especially about social problems. Thought is taken primarily for the cities when perhaps it isn't the cities that so much matter. Smart plays are written for blasé audiences in a metropolis; eccentric poetry and clever novels are concocted about dwellers in crowded streets who, poor souls, are cut off through most of the year from contact with the soil, the woods, and the sea, and who perhaps never did a day's hard manual labor in their lives; and to whom the very changes of the weather are but feebly perceptible. They are deprived of that discipline which is imposed by daily contact with the leisurely growth of crops, by the anxiety that those crops should be so at the mercy of nature's caprice, and yet also the reassuring experience of nature's bounty in the long term."

Study Questions

ORGANIZATION AND CONTENT

For many years Lucien Price recorded his conversations with Alfred North Whitehead, noted twentieth-century mathematician and philosopher. In this selection Whitehead spoke paragraphs 1, 3, and 5; Price 2 and 4.

1. What advantage do hot climates have for the development of civilization? Cold climates like Europe?
2. Is any reason given for believing that country people do better thinking than city people?
3. Why did Whitehead believe that "urbanization is a weakness..."?
4. Indicate what part of the argument is set forth in each paragraph.
5. Put the whole argument together in logical fashion.

SENTENCE STRUCTURE

1. Note that in sentences 1 and 2 the greatest emphasis is thrown on adjectives, the last words in the sentences. How is this emphasis achieved?
2. How is sentence 3 arranged so as to emphasize certain nouns?
3. What words receive chief emphasis in sentence 4?
4. Show how parallel grammatical elements function in sentence 5.
5. Rearrange sentence 5 with "European man" in other positions. What is the effect of shifting it from the final position?
6. How is contrast achieved in the sentence structure of sentence 3 of paragraph 5?
7. Explain the parallel elements of the last sentence.

DICTION

1. Look up *staple* (noun), *stultifies, proliferation, elemental, urbanization, blasé, metropolis, eccentric, concocted, discipline, caprice.*
2. What is the common element in *proliferate, prolific,* and *proletariat?*
3. What other words are based on the root of *urbanization? Metropolis? Eccentric?*

ASSIGNMENT

Perhaps you would like to argue on the other side from Whitehead—that city people have advantages over country people for the advance of civilization. Present evidence in two paragraphs.

You might argue in more detail that nature's influence is good for a person; or, on the other side, that nature has an unfavorable influence.

Perhaps you might show why you believe that some other region—the Pacific Coast, the South, or New England—is more likely to be the seat of a great civilization than the Midwest. Be sure to present your evidence in a logical and orderly manner.

PROOF OF MAN'S EARLY MANIFESTATIONS OF RELIGION
by Andre Senet (Malcolm Barnes, trans.)

1 Religious manifestations are found first of all in the cult of the dead. Very often, in fact, the skeletons or fragments of skeletons that have been discovered were beyond doubt deliberately buried. Examples are abundant. The Neanderthal man of La Chapellaux-Saints (1908) was buried in a geometrically shaped grave; the men discovered in 1909 by Peyrony and Capitan at La Ferrassie in Dordogne were all buried in specially dug graves, surrounded by offerings of food, as evidenced by the presence of pieces of animal skeletons. Again, the skeleton of a Neanderthal man was discovered in the Hissar Mountains of Siberia, north of the town of Baissoum, and around it were disposed in a regular fashion the tops of the skulls of goat-like ruminants, still with their horns. At Solutre, in the department of Saone-et-Loire, five skeletons were found buried parallel to one another. Further, like the Red Lady of Paviland and all the Grimaldi skeletons, there was red ochre on numerous skeletons, probably the symbolic representation of blood. At Grimaldi, too, a blue stone was placed upon the middle of the old woman's forehead. In the Trou Violet cave in the Pyrenees pebbles were disposed in such a way as to outline the body of the dead person.

2 All these facts show beyond dispute that the Neanderthal men and the men of the Reindeer Age had practised a cult of the dead. Moreover, it is not uncommon to find skeletons with their limbs folded back along the body in the position called "fetal," because it recalls the position of the fetus in the womb. Indeed, in order that they should keep this position for ever, the corpses

had had to be placed folded and then tied: perhaps because the fear of death obliged men to bind the bodies and so render them inoffensive, perhaps also because there was a quite simple wish to give parents or friends the ideal position of rest and sleep, and perhaps, finally, because by giving the dead man a fetal posture it was made possible for him to be born again. This last hypothesis brings us to the idea of survival, which was certainly not strange to some peoples of the Upper Paleolithic. It is to this idea of survival that one must attribute the presence of tools, weapons, food-stuffs, decorative objects, and so on around many skeletons. It is probably to this idea, too, that one must relate the symbolic representation of blood in the form of red ochre. But, whatever the hypothesis, it is nevertheless clear that the existence of a funerary cult among prehistoric men is beyond dispute and that it goes back at least some 75,000 years.

Study Questions

ORGANIZATION AND CONTENT

1. The first three sentences of paragraph 1 evidently go together. Explain how they are logically connected.
2. In sentences 4–9 several facts are presented. What do all these facts have in common?
3. How are sentences 4–9 related to sentence 3?
4. What is the function of paragraph 2, sentence 1? Is it the topic sentence?
5. What additional facts are presented in paragraph 2?
6. What do these facts, taken with those of paragraph 1, demonstrate to the reader?
7. Which sentences in the two paragraphs state what things are being proved?
8. Point out what linking (transitional) terms are used.

SENTENCE STRUCTURE

1. By what varied means does the author mention the places in which ancient skeletons have been found?
2. Does mention of each location occur in the same place in each sentence?
3. Why does the author think he must mention these locations?
4. In paragraph 2, sentence 3, the author says that something was

done "because" of certain reasons; how are the reasons organized in the sentence?

5. Sentences 5 and 6 both begin with *it*. What does the *it* refer to?
6. Why does the last sentence begin with *but?*

DICTION

1. Look up *manifestations, Neanderthal, ruminants, fetal, hypothesis, Paleolithic, funerary, prehistoric.*
2. Show the original meaning of each part of each word.

ASSIGNMENT

Place yourself in the position of someone who says, "Yes, there is evidence on this question, and the evidence shows this." You will have to do some preparation, of course, before you can write a similar paragraph presenting evidence for proof. Try to answer the question:

1. How much education is necessary for success? It will become more manageable if you ask how much education is necessary for success in various fields at various times. Take samples of people listed in *The Dictionary of National Biography, The Dictionary of American Biography, Who's Who, Who's Who in America.* The samples will provide data on the question. Use certain specific examples to prove your point.
2. Did it seem probable in the years just before 1939 that war would break out in Europe? Check magazines of the 1930's and some history books for evidence. Present the evidence in one or two paragraphs.
3. What things do certain animals or birds eat? Read works in which evidence is presented regarding the food habits of these creatures, and show in a paragraph or two what these studies prove.

WHY SAVAGES ACQUIRE EXTENSIVE KNOWLEDGE *by John Wilson*

1 If you would see the most extensive acquisition of knowledge enforced by the necessities of life, you must know what is the life of a savage, in those tribes where there is full power of mind, for

John Wilson, *Noctes Ambrosianae*, Vol. IV (New York, 1863).

in some the mind is extraordinarily degraded. For example, many of the tribes of the North American Indians, before they were visited with the curse of an intercourse with Europeans, possessed a high character of mind, both for heroic and intellectual qualities. Now, conceive one of these Indians cast amidst the boundlessness of nature—with a mind strong and ardent—not beginning life as we do—surrounded with a thousand helps to guard it from all sufferings and necessities, to spare it all use of its faculties—but cast upon the bosom of nature—to win from her the means of the preservation of his existence. From the moment he begins to understand and know—he sees what the course of his life is to be. He is to be a hunter and an inhabitant of the woods. Now, imagine all the multitude of natural facts, on the knowledge of which, for safety and sustenance, his mind is made to rest. He is a hunter—that is to say, that from the day he can use his hands at his will, he will begin his warfare against the animal race. What does that mean? That of every bird and animal of which his power can compass the destruction, he must begin to know the signs, the haunts, and the ways. He is already engaged as an observer in natural history. You may be sure he has very soon as exact a knowledge of the figure, colours, cries, &c., of many of them, and of the place and construction of the habitations of those which find, or make themselves habitations—of their young, or eggs—their number, their seasons, and precautions of breeding, &c., as any naturalist from Linnæus to Cuvier. Now, every thing he has to do to ensnare, entice, waylay them, is drawn entirely from observation of the various particulars of their modes of life. This knowledge, as he grows, he goes on extending to numbers of the birds and animals that people his dominion,—and when the savage has, by keen and extensive observation, (you have read Hearne, North!) acquired all the knowledge that affects his own well-being—of the appearance, the nature, the seasons, the modes of life of as many of these creatures as will come under the necessity or the wantonness of his art as a hunter, I ask, is it not plain that he must possess, very intimately and exactly, much of that knowledge which, when possessed by a naturalist is raised to the rank of science?

2   Combine with this the knowledge of the natural world that surrounds him, as implied by his dependence for sustenance on its

vegetable productions—and all the various knowledge of the
earth itself, and of the skies, which become important to him who
is to make his way by recollection or conjecture through un-
tracked wildernesses, forests, swamps, and precipices. How in an
unknown wilderness so made up, even after he has chosen his
course, by the stars, shall he know to trace a path through the
dangers and immensity of nature, which human feet may tread?
By observing, studying all his life long, the nature of mountains,
torrents, marshes, vegetation. Then add to this—his observation
of the air and the skies, from his dependence on their changes,
and I think, my lads, if you have imagination to represent to yourselves one-twentieth part of the knowledge which a savage will
thus be driven to possess by his mere physical necessities, you will
be astonished to find how much liker a learned man he is than you
be.

Study Questions

1. These paragraphs come from a series of imaginary conversations, the *Noctes Ambrosianae*, supposed to have taken place at
   Ambrose's Tavern in Edinburgh, and published in *Blackwood's
   Magazine* from 1822 to 1835. In the session of April, 1831, the
   conversation had got around to science and the acquisition of
   facts. What special phase of this subject is announced in the
   topic sentence of paragraph one?
2. Where does the speaker bring out a contrast between wilderness life and life in Great Britain?
3. In which sentence does the speaker make the connection between the savage Indian and science?
4. Why does he wait so long before he does this?
5. If the speaker is to make the others agree that a savage can
   acquire a great fund of knowledge (like a learned man or
   scientist), he will have to show that the savage can use something like scientific procedures. In which sentences does he do
   this? Which procedures does he mention?
6. Why does paragraph 1 end with a question?
7. In paragraph 2 greater consideration is given to what aspects
   of the study of nature than in paragraph 1?
8. What key term is repeated in the last sentence? How many

times is this term, or something very like it, used in the whole selection?

SENTENCE STRUCTURE

1. Several of the sentences are rather long, and they have a number of dashes for punctuation. What effect do the dashes have in these long sentences?
2. Which are the shortest sentences? Do the shortest sentences express some of the most important ideas or the least important?
3. How many of the sentences are interrogative?
4. Which interrogative sentences receive answers? What is the effect of using this question-and-answer technique?
5. Which sentences are periodic sentences—those in which the full meaning is held back until the reader reaches the end?
6. Has the author achieved variety of sentence structure or not?

DICTION

1. Look up *ardent, compass* (verb), *haunts* (noun), *wantonness, sustenance, torrents.*
2. Which of these words are based on Latin roots?
3. What did Linnaeus and Cuvier accomplish? What book did Samuel Hearne write about America?
4. What is the difference between *ensnare, entice,* and *waylay?* Between *recollection* and *conjecture?*
5. Does the diction of the selection produce a formal or a colloquial tone?

ASSIGNMENT

Select one of the three propositions offered and demonstrate the validity of your choice with supporting details and the reasons for your assertion.

1. A city child develops his abilities early and rapidly; or if you believe, rather, that a country child develops his abilities early and rapidly, give evidence to prove that this is so. Include some questions, as Wilson does in the selection on the savage.
2. A child is wiser than an adult. It might seem paradoxical (look up *paradox*) to assert that a child may be wiser than a grown person; Jesus, however, said, "Except ye become as little children, ye shall not enter into the kingdom of Heaven."
3. Animals may live happier lives than human beings do.

ACCEPTANCE OF LAW OR DESTRUCTION OF MANKIND
by Bertrand Russell

¹ Modern warfare, so far, has not been more destructive of life than the warfare of less scientific ages, for the increased deadliness of weapons has been offset by the improvement in medicine and hygiene. Until recent times, pestilence almost invariably proved far more fatal than enemy action. When Sennacherib besieged Jerusalem, 185,000 of his army died in one night, "and when they arose early in the morning, behold they were all dead corpses" (II Kings xix. 35). The plague in Athens did much to decide the Peloponnesian War. The many wars between Syracuse and Carthage were usually ended by pestilence. Barbarossa, after he had completely defeated the Lombard League, lost almost his whole army by disease, and had to fly secretly over the Alps. The mortality rate in such campaigns was far greater than in the two great wars of our own century. I do not say that future wars will have as low a casualty rate as the last two; that is a matter to which I will come shortly. I say only, what many people do not realize, that up to the present science has not made war more destructive.

² There are, however, other respects in which the evils of war have much increased. France was at war, almost continuously, from 1792 to 1815, and in the end suffered complete defeat, but the population of France did not, after 1815, suffer anything comparable to what has been suffered throughout Central Europe since 1945. A modern nation at war is more organized, more disciplined, and more completely concentrated on the effort to secure victory, than was possible in pre-industrial times; the consequence is that defeat is more serious, more disorganizing, more demoralizing to the general population, than it was in the days of Napoleon.

³ But even in this respect it is not possible to make a general rule. Some wars in the past were quite as disorganizing and as

destructive of the civilizations of devastated areas as was the Second World War. North Africa has never regained the level of prosperity that it enjoyed under the Romans. Persia never recovered from the Mongols nor Syria from the Turks. There have always been two kinds of wars, those in which the vanquished incurred disaster, and those in which they only incurred discomfort. We seem, unfortunately, to be entering upon an era in which wars are of the former sort.

4   The atom bomb, and still more the hydrogen bomb, have caused new fears, involving new doubts as to the effects of science on human life. Some eminent authorities, including Einstein, have pointed out that there is a danger of the extinction of all life on this planet. I do not myself think that this will happen in the next war, but I think it may well happen in the next but one, if that is allowed to occur. If this expectation is correct, we have to choose, within the next fifty years or so, between two alternatives. Either we must allow the human race to exterminate itself, or we must forgo certain liberties which are very dear to us, more especially the liberty to kill foreigners whenever we feel so disposed. I think it probable that mankind will choose its own extermination as the preferable alternative. The choice will be made, of course, by persuading ourselves that it is not being made, since (so militarists on both sides will say) the victory of the right is certain without risk of universal disaster. We are perhaps living in the last age of man, and, if so, it is to science that he will owe his extinction.

5   If, however, the human race decides to let itself go on living, it will have to make very drastic changes in its ways of thinking, feeling, and behaving. We must learn not to say: "Never! Better death than dishonor." We must learn to submit to law, even when imposed by aliens whom we hate and despise, and whom we believe to be blind to all considerations of righteousness. Consider some concrete examples. Jews and Arabs will have to agree to submit to arbitration; if the award goes against the Jews, the President of the United States will have to insure the victory of the party to which he is opposed, since, if he supports the international authority, he will lose the Jewish vote in New York State. On the other hand, if the award goes in favor of the Jews, the Mohammedan world will be indignant, and will be supported

by all other malcontents. Or, to take another instance, Eire will demand the right to oppress the Protestants of Ulster, and on this issue the United States will support Eire while Britain will support Ulster. Could an international authority survive such a dissension? Again: India and Pakistan cannot agree about Kashmir, therefore one of them must support Russia and the other the United States. It will be obvious to anyone who is an interested party in one of these disputes that the issue is far more important than the continuance of life on our planet. The hope that the human race will allow itself to survive is therefore somewhat slender.

⁶ But if human life *is* to continue in spite of science, mankind will have to learn a discipline of the passions which, in the past, has not been necessary. Men will have to submit to the law, even when they think the law unjust and iniquitous. Nations which are persuaded that they are only demanding the barest justice will have to acquiesce when this demand is denied them by the neutral authority. I do not say that this is easy; I do not prophesy that it will happen; I say only that if it does not happen the human race will perish, and will perish as a result of science.

Study Questions

ORGANIZATION AND CONTENT

1. Point out the topic sentences of paragraphs 1–3.
2. With what kind of material does Russell support the ideas in the topic sentences?
3. What points in his argument has Russell tried to make in the first three paragraphs?
4. In paragraph 1 mention is made of conditions in the past, the present, and the future. What determined the order in which the author took up these conditions?
5. What new idea is brought out in paragraph 4?
6. Note that in paragraph 4 Russell presents his readers with a dilemma (either . . . or). Explain what logical force this presentation of alternatives is intended to have.
7. What is the relation of paragraph 5 to paragraph 4?
8. Why does Russell mention the Jews, Eire, and Pakistan?
9. Paragraph 5 ends rather pessimistically; to what extent is a contrasting optimism apparent in paragraph 6?

10. Complete the following statement: The proposition that Russell is arguing may be stated as follows: . . . .
11. What issues does Russell deal with in his argument?

SENTENCE STRUCTURE

1. Russell uses few sentences in paragraph 1 in which clauses are connected with coordinating conjunctions. What purpose of this paragraph probably caused him to put sentences in the form that he used?
2. Paragraph 2 has three sentences. What considerations would determine the pattern and the length of each sentence?
3. Sentences 2 and 3 of paragraph 2 are long. Why are the sentences of paragraph 3 so much shorter?
4. Point out the ways in which transitional links are made between sentences in paragraph 4.
5. In paragraph 5 how does Russell introduce concrete examples?
6. In what different ways does he move from one concrete example to another?
7. How is a contrasting idea introduced at the beginning of paragraph 6?
8. Is sentence 2 of paragraph 6 arranged so as to provide enough emphasis?
9. The last sentence has three parts. Explain how the arrangement of words in the three parts makes this a very emphatic sentence.

DICTION

1. Are there differences of meaning between: *medicine* and *hygiene; pestilence* and *plague; mortality* and *casualty; extermination* and *extinction; dispute* and *dissension; injustice* and *iniquity?*
2. Look up *vanquished, eminent, arbitration.*
3. Is it because the extermination of the human race seems so horrible that Russell adopts an ironic tone in the second half of his argument? Consider the irony in paragraph 4 from: ". . . we must forgo certain liberties which are very dear to us, more especially the liberty to kill foreigners whenever we feel so disposed." Explain the effect of the connotations of words here which produces a shock in the last part of the sentence.
4. Similarly, when Russell says, "The choice will be made, of course. . . ," what is the effect of the "of course"?

5. What is the effect in paragraph 5 of including in one sentence: *submit, imposed, aliens, hate, despise, blind?*
6. What is the great significance of *interested party* later in paragraph 5? How does the diction of the last two sentences of paragraph 5 produce an ironic effect?

ASSIGNMENT

Write two or three paragraphs using Russell's technique of argument—an argument, that is, in terms of alternatives. Some possibilities:

1. Either we must pay college professors higher salaries, or college education will be greatly weakened.
2. Either we must admit to college all who wish to attend, or the public will remain dangerously ignorant.
3. Either we must drastically limit college admissions to the best students, or the quality of college training will be seriously diluted.
4. Either we must lessen the cost of political campaigns, or we shall be governed by rich men only.
5. Either the public must provide increased funds for medical research, or we must accept higher mortality rates for cancer and other diseases.
6. Either engineers and others with highly specialized training must have a broader education, or they will be unable to participate in our public life.
7. Either we must admit more foreign students to our colleges and send more of our native students abroad, or expect that effective international understanding will be dangerously delayed.

Be sure to support the issues of your argument with good evidence.

AN AGE OF INTROVERSION IS NOT BAD *by Ralph Waldo Emerson*

Our age is bewailed as the age of Introversion. Must that needs be evil? We, it seems, are critical; we are embarrassed with second thoughts; we cannot enjoy anything for hankering to

Ralph Waldo Emerson, "The American Scholar," in *Nature, Addresses, and Lectures* (Boston, 1892).

know whereof the pleasure consists; we are lined with eyes; we see with our feet; the time is infected with Hamlet's unhappiness,—

> "Sicklied o'er with the pale cast of thought."

Is it so bad then? Sight is the last thing to be pitied. Would we be blind? Do we fear lest we should outsee nature and God, and drink truth dry? I look upon the discontent of the literary class, as a mere announcement of the fact, that they find themselves not in the state of mind of their fathers, and regret the coming state as untried; as a boy dreads the water before he has learned that he can swim. If there is any period one would desire to be born in,—is it not the age of Revolution; when the old and the new stand side by side, and admit of being compared; when the energies of all men are searched by fear and by hope; when the historic glories of the old can be compensated by the rich possibilities of the new era? This time like all times, is a very good one, if we but know what to do with it.

Study Questions

ORGANIZATION AND CONTENT

1. What is the topic sentence of the paragraph?
2. Where does Emerson state the point of view of his opposition?
3. There are four questions among the first seven sentences. What is the function of these questions? How are they to be answered?
4. "Seeing" in sentence 3 is equated with what? What less desirable alternative does Emerson suggest to seeing?
5. What has Emerson accomplished for his argument in the first seven sentences?
6. What new phase of the argument is developed in sentences 8–9?
7. Explain the analogy in sentence 8.
8. How is the last clause of the paragraph—"if we but know what to do with it"—related to the preceding material?
9. Complete this sentence: According to Emerson, an age of introversion is not bad because . . .

SENTENCE STRUCTURE

1. Sentence 3 has six parts; are they all parallel? Where is parallel phrasing used?

2. To what extent is repetition used in sentence 3?
3. How are parts 4 and 5 of sentence 3 different in expression from parts 1-3?
4. Would it be better to place the *Hamlet* quotation elsewhere in the sentence?
5. Sentence 9 has several contrasts; point them out.
6. In what terms are these contrasts indicated in sentence 8?

DICTION

1. Look up *introversion.*
2. What verbs are most effective in sentence 3?
3. Point out metaphors in sentence 3.
4. Like sentence 3, sentence 9 has several parts; contrast the diction of sentence 9 with that of sentence 3.

ASSIGNMENT

Write one paragraph in imitation of Emerson's, defending something against criticism. Write an argument on one of these propositions:

1. This is not a bad decade in which to live.
2. Young people today are not bad.
3. Magazines in the United States are not bad.
4. No people in the world is bad.
5. The average American home does not exhibit bad taste.

COMPULSORY ATHLETICS ARE NOT ALWAYS GOOD *by Ellery Sedgwick*

1 To make a school "tick," organized and compulsory athletics are regarded as a prime essential. Of course the normal boy—the boy to whom boarding schools are dedicated—dotes upon them. My only protest is that the odd boy, the boy who for some reason or other swims against the current and educates himself against sufficient odds, should be made subject to this tyrannous compulsion. Surely the pressure of school opinion is hydraulic enough without an official draft into universal service. If schools

are a training ground for democracy, it must be ever remembered that democracy's real test lies in its respect for minority opinion. But as a practical matter nothing simplifies a master's duties like sentencing his charges to hard, daily, and universal labor. Two hours of football practice will take the starch out of the highest spirits. It may dull a boy's intellectual capacities, but it makes him docile as a sheep. Exhausted boys are good boys: that is no secret in any dormitory. But to be fair to masters, I do not believe it often occurs to them how useful compulsory athletics are to their professional convenience. They take them as a matter of course, honestly believing that the school team is an embodiment of the spirit of the school. All for one and one for all seems to them the exemplification of the very ideal they strive for. And younger masters especially are apt to share the astonishing belief that moral courage is a by-product of the physical struggle, that it fosters all the nobler virtues. The probability that it may tend to atrophy the brain is never discussed at faculty meetings. Organized sport is the personification of manliness. The boy who seeks another road to his development presents to the master a picture of a shirker and not infrequently of a poltroon as well. And from the boys themselves, masters half accept the quaint idea that victory for the team is an added glory to the school.

2 I do not wish to be misunderstood. Teams should play and play to win. But boys to whom the whole idea of organized athletics is depressing should be allowed to go their several ways and no blight of recognized eccentricity should fall upon them. The records of after life seem to bear me out. It has not been my experience that boys who have worn school letters on their sweaters and whose names have rung out across gridiron or diamond at the end of nine hurrahs are a whit more likely to have the moral courage which active life demands than those nonconformists who have climbed their own lonely staircases to positions of responsibility. I will go further and say that even in physical courage the heroes of boyhood do not always put up a better front in times of later danger. Determination, character we call it, comes by devious and difficult roads. Many of these routes are unsurveyed and where is the guide who can lead straight to the goal that every father seeks for his boy!

Study Questions

ORGANIZATION AND CONTENT

1. Complete the following statement: The specific proposition being argued in this selection is . . .
2. We can perceive at least three issues in this argument. How would you phrase the issue in terms of "the odd boy"? Of "intellectual capacities"? Of "character"? Try to be exact.
3. According to the author, what is the opposing contention on each issue?
4. What evidence is given in support of each issue?
5. Are all the issues equally well supported? If not, which issue receives the best support? The poorest support?
6. Distinguish paragraph 2 from paragraph 1 in terms of content.

SENTENCE STRUCTURE

1. Both sentences 2 and 3 of paragraph 1 have an interruptive appositive element in the middle. Is there any reason why they should not be punctuated in the same way?
2. To what extent are these two sentences similar in both phrasing and construction? In what respects do they contrast?
3. Which sentences of paragraph 1 are the shortest? What is the effect of their shortness?
4. Sentences 6, 10, 13, and 17 begin with coordinating conjunctions. Why?
5. Which sentences of paragraph 2 are the shortest? What is the effect of their shortness?

DICTION

1. Look up *essential, docile, exemplification, atrophy, personification, poltroon, devious.*
2. Which of these words come to English from Latin or Greek?
3. Learn the meanings of their roots.
4. Explain the effect in the argument of certain phrases: "tyrannous compulsion" (sentence 3), "sentencing . . . to hard, daily, and universal labor" (sentence 6), "docile as a sheep" (sentence 8), "poltroon" (sentence 16), "quaint idea" (sentence 17), "blight of recognized eccentricity" (paragraph 2, sentence 3), "their own lonely staircases" (paragraph 2, sentence 5).
5. Has the author used the connotations of these terms to take an unfair advantage in the argument?

6. Is Sedgwick's style too formal? Too informal? Too much a mixture of the formal and the informal? (Consider the different effects of "take the starch out of" [sentence 7] and "tend to atrophy the brain" [sentence 14]; of "put up a better front" [paragraph 2, sentence 6] and "comes by devious and difficult roads" [paragraph 2, sentence 7].)

ASSIGNMENT

State the proposition and the issues for an argument in one or two paragraphs on one of the following topics, and then write the argument in imitation of Sedgwick's.

1. Compulsory college courses are not always good.
2. Certain groups should not be allowed to vote (or should be allowed only half a vote each).
3. Americans are not conspicuously honest (or intelligent, or imaginative, or artistic).
4. Fraternity or sorority membership is not desirable.
5. It would be unwise, in the United States, to forbid freedom of speech to anyone.

IN FAVOR OF CATHOLIC EMANCIPATION *by Sydney Smith*

No Catholic can be chief Governor or Governor of this Kingdom, Chancellor or Keeper of the Great Seal, Lord High Treasurer, Chief of any of the Courts of Justice, Chancellor of the Exchequer, Puisne Judge, Judge in the Admiralty, Master of the Rolls, Secretary of State, Keeper of the Privy Seal, Vice-Treasurer or his Deputy, Teller or Cashier of Exchequer, Auditor or General, Governor or Custos Rotulorum of Counties, Chief Governor's Secretary, Privy Councillor, King's Counsel, Sergeant, Attorney, Solicitor-General, Master in Chancery, Provost or Fellow of Trinity College, Dublin, Postmaster-General, Master and Lieutenant-General of Ordnance, Commander-in-Chief, General on the Staff, Sheriff, Sub-Sheriff, Mayor, Bailiff, Recorder, Burgess, or any other officer in a City, or a Corporation. No Catholic can be guardian to a Protestant, and no priest guardian

Sydney Smith, *The Peter Plymley Letters* (1807).

at all: no Catholic can be a gamekeeper, or have for sale, or otherwise, any arms or warlike stores: no Catholic can present to a living, unless he choose to turn Jew in order to obtain that privilege; the pecuniary qualification of Catholic jurors is made higher than that of Protestants, and no relaxation of the ancient rigorous code is permitted, unless to those who shall take an oath prescribed by 13 & 14 Geo. III. Now if this is not picking the plums out of the pudding, and leaving the mere batter to the Catholics, I know not what is. If it were merely the Privy Council, it would be (I allow) nothing but a point of honour for which the mass of Catholics were contending; the honour of being chief-mourners or pall-bearers to the country; but surely no man will contend that every barrister may not speculate upon the possibility of being a puisne Judge; and that every shopkeeper must not feel himself injured by his exclusion from borough offices.

Study Questions

ORGANIZATION AND CONTENT

This paragraph is taken from *The Peter Plymley Letters*, written in 1807 by Sydney Smith, a clergyman of the Church of England and one of the founders of *The Edinburgh Review*. The restrictions on English Catholics which Smith enumerates were not finally removed until Parliament passed the Catholic Emancipation Act in 1829.

1. This paragraph consists of four sentences. What are the differences in content between sentences 1 and 2 and sentences 3 and 4?
2. In what way does the material in sentence 2 differ from that in sentence 1?
3. On the basis of this paragraph, how would you state the proposition that Smith is arguing?
4. With what issue does this paragraph deal?
5. Does Smith use effective evidence for his argument?
6. To what extent does he make use of reasoning?
7. What assumptions would you judge that Smith has made?

SENTENCE STRUCTURE

1. Sentence 1 is very long and sentence 2 is long. By what means has the author made them long?

2. Explain the effect of these two sentences in terms of argument.
3. Explain the effect of the change of length and of tone that occurs in sentence 3.
4. How does sentence 4 differ in tone and structure from sentence 3?

DICTION

1. Look up *chancellor, exchequer, puisne, privy, teller, auditor, Chancery, provost, ordnance, bailiff, pecuniary, rigorous, barrister.*
2. What does "present to a living" (sentence 2) mean?
3. Explain the relation between *puisne* and *puny, burgess* and *borough.*
4. How do the connotations of words in sentence 3 give it a different effect from that of the other sentences?

ASSIGNMENT

Imitate the paragraph of Smith by writing a paragraph composed of four similar sentences trying to convince a reader that some group is being discriminated against—for example, Negroes, union members, nonunion members, Mexicans, women, Puerto Ricans, uneducated persons, conservatives, liberals, Catholics, persons educated in the liberal arts.

ROMANCE IS A POOR BASIS FOR MARRIAGE *by Denis de Rougemont* (*Montgomery Belgion, trans.*)

1 The better to see our situation, let us look at America—that other Europe which has been released from both the routine practices and traditional restraints of the old. No other known civilization, in the 7,000 years that one civilization has been succeeding another, has bestowed on the love known as *romance* anything like the same amount of daily publicity by means of the screen, the hoarding, the letter-press and advertisements in maga-

zines, by means of songs and pictures, and of current morals and of whatever defies them. No other civilization has embarked with anything like the same ingenuous assurance upon the perilous enterprise of making marriage coincide with love thus understood, and of making the first depend upon the second.

² During a telephone strike in 1947, the women operators in the county town of White Plains, near New York, received the following call: "My girl and I want to get married. We're trying to locate a justice of the peace. Is it an emergency?" The women telephone operators decided forthwith that it was. And the newspaper which reported the item headed it: "Love is Classified as an Emergency." This commonplace newspaper cutting provides an example of the perfectly natural beliefs of Americans, and that is how it is of interest. It shows that in America the terms "love" and "marriage" are practically equivalent; that when one "loves" one must get married instantly; and, further, that "love" should normally overcome all obstacles, as is shown every day in films, novels, and comic-strips. In reality, however, let romantic love overcome no matter how many obstacles, and it almost always fails at one. That is the obstacle constituted by time. Now, either marriage is an institution set up to be lasting—or it is meaningless. That is the first secret of the present breakdown, a breakdown of which the extent can be measured simply by reference to divorce statistics, where the United States heads the list of countries. To try to base marriage on a form of love which is unstable by definition is really to benefit the State of Nevada. To insist that no matter what film, even one about the atomic bomb, shall contain a certain amount of the romantic drug—and romantic more than erotic—known as "love interest," is to give publicity to the germs that are making marriage ill, not to a cure.

³ Romance feeds on obstacles, short excitations, and partings; marriage, on the contrary, is made up of wont, daily propinquity, growing accustomed to one another. Romance calls for "the faraway love" of the troubadours; marriage, for love of "one's neighbour." Where, then, a couple have married in obedience to a romance, it is natural that the first time a conflict of temperament or of taste becomes manifest the parties should each ask themselves: "Why did I marry?" And it is no less natural that, obsessed by the universal propaganda in favour of romance, each

should seize the first occasion to fall in love with somebody else. And thereupon it is perfectly logical to decide to divorce, so as to obtain from the new love, which demands a fresh marriage, a new promise of happiness—all three words, "marriage," "love," "happiness," being synonyms. Thus, remedying boredom with a passing fever, "he for the second time, she for the fourth," American men and women go in quest of "adjustment." They do not seek it, however, in the old situation, the one guaranteed—"for better, for worse"—by a vow. They seek it, on the contrary, in a fresh "experience" regarded as such, and affected from the start by the same potentialities of failure as those which preceded it. That is how divorce assumes in the United States a less "disastrous" character, and is even more "normal," than in Europe. There where a European regards the rupture of a marriage as producing social disorder and the loss of a capital of joint recollections and experiences, an American has rather the impression that "he is putting his life straight," and opening up for himself a fresh future. The economy of saving is once again opposed to that of squandering, as the concern to preserve the past is opposed to the concern to make a clean sweep in order to build something tidy, without compromise. But any man opposed to compromise is inconsistent in marrying. And he who would draw a draft on his future is very unwise to mention beforehand that he wishes to be allowed not to honour it; as did the young millionairess who told the newspaper men on the eve of her marriage: "It's marvellous to be getting married *for the first time!*" A year later, she got divorced.

⁴   Whereupon a number of people propose to forbid divorce, or at least to render it very difficult. But it is marriage which, in my opinion, has been made too easy, through the supposition that let there be "love" and marriage should follow, regardless of outmoded conventions of social and religious station, of upbringing and substance. It is certainly possible to imagine new conditions which candidates for marriage—that true "co-existence" which should be enduring, peaceable, and mutually educative—should fulfil. It is possible to exact tests or ordeals bearing on whatever gives any human union its best chances of lasting: aims in life, rhythms of life, comparative vocations, characters, and temperaments. If marriage—that is to say, lastingness—is what is wanted,

it is natural to ensure its conditions. But such reforms would have little effect in a world which retained, if not true passion, at least the nostalgia of passion that has grown congenital in Western man.

⁵ When marriage was established on social conventions, and hence, from the individual standpoint, on chance, it had at least as much likelihood of success as marriage based on "love" alone. But the whole of Western evolution goes from tribal wisdom to individual risk; it is irreversible, and it must be approved to the extent it tends to make collective and native destiny depend on personal decision.

Study Questions

ORGANIZATION AND CONTENT

1. Why does the author focus paragraph 1 on America?
2. Why does he tell the story of the telephone operators in paragraph 2? Which sentence brings out his purpose?
3. In the second half of paragraph 2, what objection to romance does the author raise?
4. In sentence 10 of paragraph 2, what effect in the argument does the *either–or* statement have? Is it acceptable to you?
5. Paragraph 3 points out contrasts. List them.
6. Paragraph 4 shows the author rather dubious about reforms. Why?
7. To what extent does the author make concessions in paragraph 5?
8. The author makes use of specific examples, of definitions, of reasoning from assumptions. Which of these means of argument is the most effective?
9. In what terms does the author define *romance* and *marriage*?
10. How are America and Europe represented? Does the effectiveness of the argument depend at all upon one's attitude toward America or Europe?
11. Set down De Rougemont's argument in the form of a syllogism, with major premise, minor premise, and conclusion.

SENTENCE STRUCTURE

1. Explain the reason for the structure of sentences 1 and 2 of paragraph 3.

2. Indicate by what means sentences 3–6 of paragraph 3 are linked.
3. What terms show that the author in sentences 3–6 is drawing conclusions from the ideas in sentences 1 and 2 of paragraph 3?
4. Why is the last sentence of paragraph 3 so short?
5. Are there too many "interrupters" in the sentences of paragraph 4?

DICTION

1. Look up *romance, hoarding, ingenuous, erotic, wont, propinquity, troubadour, obsessed, economy, nostalgia, congenital.*
2. Why do so many words have quotation marks around them?
3. Which of De Rougemont's terms are metaphors?

ASSIGNMENT

De Rougemont's argument may make you wish to reply to it by writing a defense of marriage based on romance. If you choose to do so, state clearly on what issues you base your counterargument.

Perhaps you prefer to imitate the work of De Rougemont in an argument that says *this* is better than (or preferable to) *that*. Some possibilities:

1. A campus with plenty of grass and trees and without automobiles is preferable to a campus with large areas given up to parking lots and many automobiles.
2. It is better to read much (100 books a year, for example) than to read little, as most Americans do.
3. It is better to play a musical instrument (or sing) than to attend concerts.
4. For nonscience students it would be better to read books about the history of science and the significance of science than to take a course in laboratory science.

WHY AN ESTABLISHED RELIGION MUST HAVE SHORTCOMINGS *by Soame Jenyns*

An Established Religion must be liable to many imperfections from its own nature, and the nature of man; in its original constitution, it must lean to the errors and prejudices of the times;

Soame Jenyns, *Works* (London, 1790).

and, how much soever it is then approved, it cannot long preserve that approbation, because, human science being continually fluctuating, mankind grow more or less knowing in every generation, and consequently must change their opinions on religious, as well as on all other subjects; so that however wisely any Established System may be formed at first, it must, from the natural increase of human knowledge, be found or thought to be erroneous in the course of a few years: and yet the change of national religions cannot keep pace with the alterations of national opinions, because such frequent reviews and reformations would totally unhinge men's principles, and subvert the foundations of all religion and morality whatever. It must likewise be corrupted by the very establishment which protects it, because by that it will be mixed with the worldly pursuits of its degenerate votaries; and it must be extremely dissimilar to its original purity, or it would be incapable of being established; for pure and genuine Christianity never was, nor ever can be the National Religion of any country upon earth. It is a gold too refined to be worked up with any human institution, without a large portion of alloy; for, no sooner is this small grain of mustard seed watered with the fertile showers of civil emoluments, than it grows up into a large and spreading tree, under the shelter of whose branches the birds of prey and plunder will not fail to make for themselves comfortable habitations, and thence deface its beauty and destroy its fruits.

Study Questions

ORGANIZATION AND CONTENT

1. Be sure you know what is meant by an Established Religion.
2. State the proposition that Jenyns is arguing.
3. State the two issues on which he undertakes to convince us.
4. What is the function of the statement in sentence 1 immediately after the colon—"and yet the change . . ."?
5. How does sentence 2 support the argument? Does it have any connection with sentence 1?
6. In what way does sentence 3 have a bearing on the discussion?
7. Sentence 3 mentions gold, mustard seed, and a tree; of what use are they in the argument? Are they metaphors, analogies, illustrations, data, evidence, or historical examples?

SENTENCE STRUCTURE

1. Is any of the three sentences of the paragraph too long?
2. Though the sentences have several parts, by what means has the author tried to make them easy to understand?
3. What principle of structure do all three sentences follow?
4. This paragraph was written in the eighteenth century. Would a twentieth-century writer write the sentences in any different way?

DICTION

1. Look up *approbation, science, fluctuating, erroneous, subvert, degenerate votaries, civil emoluments.*
2. From what language do these words come? Judging by his vocabulary and sentence structure, what would you suppose about the author's education?
3. Does the author use a learned or a popular vocabulary?
4. Which sentence contains the greatest number of concrete terms?
5. What are the connotations of "fertile showers," "prey and plunder," "deface . . . and destroy"?

ASSIGNMENT

Write one or two paragraphs in which you convince a reader why, under given conditions, a certain thing was bound to happen. Some suggestions:

1. Why the number of people engaged in farming in the United States declined in the twentieth century
2. Why railroads in the United States are a declining industry
3. Why California has grown rapidly in population
4. Why many American college students are poorly prepared for college
5. Why American mass-produced articles have shortcomings
6. Why your Church has shortcomings
7. Why your college has shortcomings
8. Why the people of a region (South, East, West) have developed certain recognizable qualities

Remember that you do not have to demonstrate that the thing has happened but to convince a reader why it had to happen.

THE SIZE OF THE UNITED STATES SENATE AND THE TERMS OF THE SENATORS *by James Madison*

1   IV. The number of senators and the duration of their appointment come next to be considered. In order to form an accurate judgment on both these points it will be proper to inquire into the purposes which are to be answered by a senate; and in order to ascertain these it will be necessary to review the inconveniences which a republic must suffer from the want of such an institution.

2   *First.* It is a misfortune incident to republican government, though in a less degree than to other governments, that those who administer it may forget their obligations to their constituents and prove unfaithful to their important trust. In this point of view, a senate, as a second branch of the legislative assembly, distinct from, and dividing the power with, a first, must be in all cases a salutary check on the government. It doubles the security to the people by requiring the concurrence of two distinct bodies in schemes of usurpation or perfidy, where the ambition or corruption of one would otherwise be sufficient. This is a precaution founded on such clear principles, and now so well understood in the United States, that it would be more than superfluous to enlarge on it. I will barely remark that, as the improbability of sinister combinations will be in proportion to the dissimilarity in the genius of the two bodies, it must be politic to distinguish them from each other by every circumstance which will consist with a due harmony in all proper measures and with the genuine principles of republican government.

3   *Secondly.* The necessity of a senate is not less indicated by the propensity of all single and numerous assemblies to yield to the impulse of sudden and violent passions and to be seduced by factious leaders into intemperate and pernicious resolutions. Examples on this subject might be cited without number, and from proceedings within the United States as well as from the history of other nations. But a position that will not be contradicted need

Alexander Hamilton, James Madison, and John Jay, *The Federalist* (1788).

not be proved. All that need be remarked is that a body which is to correct this infirmity ought itself to be free from it, and consequently ought to be less numerous. It ought, moreover, to possess great firmness, and consequently ought to hold its authority by a tenure of considerable duration.

⁴ *Thirdly.* Another defect to be supplied by a senate lies in a want of due acquaintance with the objects and principles of legislation. It is not possible that an assembly of men called for the most part from pursuits of a private nature, continued in appointment for a short time and led by no permanent motive to devote the intervals of public occupation to a study of the laws, the affairs, and the comprehensive interests of their country, should, if left wholly to themselves, escape a variety of important errors in the exercise of their legislative trust. It may be affirmed, on the best grounds, that no small share of the present embarrassments of America is to be charged on the blunders of our governments, and that these have proceeded from the heads rather than the hearts of most of the authors of them. What indeed are all the repealing, explaining, and amending laws, which fill and disgrace our voluminous codes, but so many monuments of deficient wisdom, so many impeachments exhibited by each succeeding against each preceding session, so many admonitions to the people of the value of those aids which may be expected from a well-constituted senate?

⁵ A good government implies two things: first, fidelity to the object of government, which is the happiness of the people; secondly, a knowledge of the means by which that object can be best attained. Some governments are deficient in both these qualities, most governments are deficient in the first. I scruple not to assert that in American governments too little attention has been paid to the last. The federal Constitution avoids this error; and what merits particular notice, it provides for the last in a mode which increases the security for the first.

⁶ *Fourthly.* The mutability in the public councils arising from a rapid succession of new members, however qualified they may be, points out, in the strongest manner, the necessity of some stable institution in the government. Every new election in the States is found to change one half of the representatives. From this change of men must proceed a change of opinions; and from

a change of opinions, a change of measures. But a continual change even of good measures is inconsistent with every rule of prudence and every prospect of success. The remark is verified in private life and becomes more just, as well as more important, in national transactions. . . .

⁷ A *fifth* desideratum illustrating the utility of a senate is the want of a due sense of national character. Without a select and stable member of the government, the esteem of foreign powers will not only be forfeited by an unenlightened and variable policy, proceeding from the causes already mentioned, but the national councils will not possess that sensibility to the opinion of the world which is perhaps not less necessary in order to merit than it is to obtain its respect and confidence.

An attention to the judgment of other nations is important to every government for two reasons: the one is that, independently of the merits of any particular plan or measure, it is desirable, on various accounts, that it should appear to other nations as the offspring of a wise and honorable policy; the second is that in doubtful cases, particularly where the national councils may be warped by some strong passion or momentary interest, the presumed or known opinion of the impartial world may be the best guide that can be followed. What has not America lost by her want of character with foreign nations, and how many errors and follies would she not have avoided if the justice and propriety of her measures had, in every instance, been previously tried by the light in which they would probably appear to the unbiased part of mankind?

⁸ Yet, however requisite a sense of national character may be, it is evident that it can never be sufficiently possessed by a numerous and changeable body. It can only be found in a number so small that a sensible degree of the praise and blame of public measures may be the portion of each individual, or in an assembly so durably invested with public trust that the pride and consequence of its members may be sensibly incorporated with the reputation and prosperity of the community. The half-yearly representatives of Rhode Island would probably have been little affected in their deliberations on the iniquitous measures of that State by arguments drawn from the light in which such measures would be viewed by foreign nations or even by the sister States,

whilst it can scarcely be doubted that if the concurrence of a select and stable body had been necessary, a regard to national character alone would have prevented the calamities under which that misguided people is now laboring.

Study Questions

ORGANIZATION AND CONTENT

1. This selection by James Madison is taken from *The Federalist*, the famous series of papers arguing for the adoption of the proposed American Constitution. In addition to the topics of discussion, what other thing is announced in paragraph 1?
2. In effect, Madison says that in order to understand A we must consider B; and in order to understand B we must consider C. What ideas do the letters represent in paragraph 1?
3. Explain what issue is discussed in each of the five parts into which Madison divides his argument.
4. In his second section Madison says that many examples might be cited from history of certain evils in legislatures. What proposal about the Senate has a bearing on these evils?
5. What makes Madison think that the Senate would pass wise laws? Is he assuming that it would pass wiser laws than the House of Representatives?
6. What bearing does the 6-year term of Senators have on the issue raised in section 4?
7. Does Madison assert in section 5 that the make-up of the Senate will have an influence on foreign nations or that foreign nations will have an influence on the Senate?
8. Does the material of section 5 support the issue of the size of the Senate or of the term of Senators?
9. Complete the following statement: According to Madison, without a Senate a republic will be likely to suffer from . . .

SENTENCE STRUCTURE

1. Is the sentence structure of the selection chiefly of a formal kind or of an informal kind?
2. Are the sentences mostly long or short? Simple or complex?
3. Analyze the structure of sentences 1 and 2 of paragraph 2.
4. The structure pattern causes what words to be emphasized in both sentences?
5. In paragraph 4 sentences 2 and 3 begin with an impersonal con-

struction. What kind of effect does this type of beginning have on the latter part of the sentence?

6. Both paragraph 4 and paragraph 8 end with questions. What effect in the argument do these questions have?
7. What word does Madison repeat in paragraph 5 in order to hold the sentences of the paragraph together?
8. Point out examples of balance in the sentences of paragraph 5.
9. Show how the sentence structure is adapted to the course of logical thought in paragraph 6.

DICTION

1. Look up *salutary, usurpation, perfidy, sinister, politic, propensity, seduced, factious, pernicious, infirmity, tenure, voluminous, impeachments, admonitions, fidelity, scruple, mutability, desideratum, sensible, durably, invested, iniquitous.*
2. Learn the meaning of the root in each of the following: *perfidy, sinister, seduced, tenure, admonitions, fidelity, mutability, sensible, durably, invested.*
3. From what language do the above words come that have three syllables or more?
4. What effect does the use of these longer words have on the style of the selection?
5. What terms would you use to describe Madison's *style?*
6. Do you think that his style was influenced most by his education, his being a lawyer, the age in which he lived (he was born in 1751), or the subject about which he was arguing?

ASSIGNMENT

Following Madison's pattern of argument, write an argument to convince a reader:

1. That everyone who studies foreign languages, science, mathematics, or English ought to pursue the study for _____ years (a considerable time)—for if he does not, then undesirable results will follow.
2. That the United States should adopt a system like that of Canada and England according to which the term of the Chief Executive (Prime Minister) may end at any time that his party loses a vote on an important issue.
3. That the President of the United States should have a longer term.
4. That students in publicly supported colleges should have all

expenses paid by the government provided that they make high scores on entrance examinations and maintain high grades in college.

5. That every citizen of the United States, before being eligible to vote in any given election, should be required to demonstrate familiarity with the issues and with the careers of the candidates.

THE VALUE OF LIBERTY
by *John Stuart Mill*

1   He who lets the world, or his own portion of it, choose his plan of life for him, has no need of any other faculty than the ape-like one of imitation. He who chooses his plan for himself, employs all his faculties. He must use observation to see, reasoning and judgment to foresee, activity to gather materials for decision, discrimination to decide, and when he has decided, firmness and self-control to hold to his deliberate decision. And these qualities he requires and exercises exactly in proportion as the part of his conduct which he determines according to his own judgment and feelings is a large one. It is possible that he might be guided in some good path, and kept out of harm's way, without any of these things. But what will be his comparative worth as a human being? It is really of importance, not only what men do, but also what manner of men they are that do it. Among the works of man, which human life is rightly employed in perfecting and beautifying, the first in importance surely is man himself. Supposing it were possible to get houses built, corn grown, battles fought, causes tried, and even churches erected and prayers said, by machinery—by automatons in human form—it would be a considerable loss to exchange for these automatons even the men and women who at present inhabit the more civilised parts of the world, and who assuredly are but starved specimens of what nature can and will produce. Human nature is not a machine to be built after a model, and set to do exactly the work prescribed for it, but a tree, which requires to grow and develop itself on all

John Stuart Mill, *On Liberty* (1859).

sides, according to the tendency of the inward forces which make it a living thing.

2   It is not by wearing down into uniformity all that is individual in themselves, but by cultivating it, and calling it forth, within the limits imposed by the rights and interests of others, that human beings become a noble and beautiful object of contemplation; and as the works partake the character of those who do them, by the same process human life also becomes rich, diversified, and animating, furnishing more abundant aliment to high thoughts and elevating feelings, and strengthening the tie which binds every individual to the race, by making the race infinitely better worth belonging to. In proportion to the development of his individuality, each person becomes more valuable to himself, and is therefore capable of being more valuable to others. There is a greater fulness of life about his own existence, and when there is more life in the units there is more in the mass which is composed of them. As much compression as is necessary to prevent the stronger specimens of human nature from encroaching on the rights of others cannot be dispensed with; but for this there is ample compensation even in the point of view of human development. The means of development which the individual loses by being prevented from gratifying his inclinations to the injury of others, are chiefly obtained at the expense of the development of other people. And even to himself there is a full equivalent in the better development of the social part of his nature, rendered possible by the restraint put upon the selfish part. To be held to rigid rules of justice for the sake of others, develops the feelings and capacities which have the good of others for their object. But to be restrained in things not affecting their good, by their mere displeasure, develops nothing valuable, except such force of character as may unfold itself in resisting the restraint. If acquiesced in, it dulls and blunts the whole nature. To give any fair play to the nature of each, it is essential that different persons should be allowed to lead different lives. In proportion as this latitude has been exercised in any age, has that age been noteworthy to posterity. Even despotism does not produce its worst effects, so long as individuality exists under it; and whatever crushes individuality is despotism, by whatever name it may be called, and whether it professes to be enforcing the will of God or the injunctions of men.

3   Having said that the individuality is the same thing with development, and that it is only the cultivation of individuality which produces, or can produce, well-developed human beings, I might here close the argument: for what more or better can be said of any condition of human affairs than that it brings human beings themselves nearer to the best thing they can be? Or what worse can be said of any obstruction to good than that it prevents this? Doubtless, however, these considerations will not suffice to convince those who most need convincing; and it is necessary further to show, that these developed human beings are of some use to the undeveloped—to point out to those who do not desire liberty, and would not avail themselves of it, that they may be in some intelligible manner rewarded for allowing other people to make use of it without hindrance.

4   In the first place, then, I would suggest that they might possibly learn something from them. It will not be denied by anybody, that originality is a valuable element in human affairs. There is always need of persons not only to discover new truths, and point out when what were once truths are true no longer, but also to commence new practices, and set the example of more enlightened conduct, and better taste and sense in human life. This cannot well be gainsaid by anybody who does not believe that the world has already attained perfection in all its ways and practices. It is true that this benefit is not capable of being rendered by everybody alike: there are but few persons, in comparison with the whole of mankind, whose experiments, if adopted by others, would be likely to be any improvement on established practice. But these few are the salt of the earth; without them, human life would become a stagnant pool. Not only is it they who introduce good things which did not before exist; it is they who keep the life in those which already exist. If there were nothing new to be done, would human intellect cease to be necessary? Would it be a reason why those who do the old things should forget why they are done, and do them like cattle, not like human beings? There is only too great a tendency in the best beliefs and practices to degenerate into the mechanical; and unless there were a succession of persons whose ever-recurring originality prevents the grounds of those beliefs and practices from becoming merely traditional, such dead matter would not resist the smallest shock from anything really alive, and there would be no reason why

civilisation should not die out, as in the Byzantine Empire. Persons of genius, it is true, are, and are always likely to be, a small minority; but in order to have them, it is necessary to preserve the soil in which they grow. Genius can only breathe freely in an *atmosphere* of freedom. Persons of genius are, *ex vi termini*, more individual than any other people—less capable, consequently, of fitting themselves, without hurtful compression, into any of the small number of moulds which society provides in order to save its members the trouble of forming their own character. If from timidity they consent to be forced into one of these moulds, and to let all that part of themselves which cannot expand under the pressure remain unexpanded, society will be little the better for their genius. If they are of a strong character, and break their fetters, they become a mark for the society which has not succeeded in reducing them to commonplace, to point out with solemn warning as "wild," "erratic," and the like; much as if one should complain of the Niagara River for not flowing smoothly between its banks like a Dutch canal.

⁵ I insist thus emphatically on the importance of genius, and the necessity of allowing it to unfold itself freely both in thought and in practice, being well aware that no one will deny the position in theory, but knowing also that almost every one, in reality, is totally indifferent to it. People think genius a fine thing if it enables a man to write an exciting poem, or paint a picture. But in its true sense, that of originality in thought and action, though no one says that it is not a thing to be admired, nearly all, at heart, think that they can do very well without it. Unhappily this is too natural to be wondered at. Originality is the one thing which unoriginal minds cannot feel the use of. They cannot see what it is to do for them: how should they? If they could see what it would do for them, it would not be originality. The first service which originality has to render them, is that of opening their eyes: which being once fully done, they would have a chance of being themselves original. Meanwhile, recollecting that nothing was ever yet done which some one was not the first to do, and that all good things which exist are the fruits of originality, let them be modest enough to believe that there is something still left for it to accomplish, and assure themselves that they are more in need of originality, the less they are conscious of the want.

Study Questions

ORGANIZATION AND CONTENT

1. In what sentences of paragraph 1 is the topic expressed?
2. What is the significance of the question in the middle of paragraph 1?
3. In the latter part of paragraph 1 Mill makes reference to machinery and a tree. How do these references help his argument?
4. Does paragraph 2 have a topic sentence?
5. What are the key words of paragraph 2?
6. In sentence 4 of paragraph 2 Mill seems to agree to some restrictions upon liberty. How can he justify such restrictions?
7. In his opinion what restrictions cannot be permitted?
8. What is the purpose of paragraph 3?
9. What issue is Mill trying to prove in paragraph 4?
10. According to Mill in paragraph 4, the loss of liberty would produce what bad effects?
11. In sentence 6 of paragraph 4 Mill uses metaphors of salt and of a pool. Explain them.
12. How does the point of paragraph 5 differ from that of paragraph 4?
13. Complete this statement: According to Mill everybody should grant freedom to other people because . . .

SENTENCE STRUCTURE

1. How is sentence 2 of paragraph 1 arranged so as to emphasize a contrast with sentence 1?
2. In sentence 3 a number of qualities and activities are listed. What grammatical relationship governs the list, and what determines the order of the list?
3. Sentence 9 is an interesting one. The infinitive *to get* has six objects (why is it effective to list so many separate things?), and the introductory dependent clause ends with the phrase *by machinery;* then, after the appositive set off by dashes comes the main clause. In the main clause what terms contrast with *machinery?* Why is it effective to end the dependent clause with *machinery?* Why is it skillful for Mill to place the phrase *for these automatons* directly after *to exchange?* Why does Mill wish to end his sentence with the two *who-*clauses modifying *men* and *women?* What important contrast is brought out by these parallel *who-*clauses? How many

words does sentence 9 contain? Mill's arrangement of these words is a brilliant example of sentence management.

4. Show how sentence 10 uses the principle of contrast; of emphasis.
5. Explain the problems involved in the management of sentence 1 of paragraph 2.
6. Show how the two interrogative sentences of paragraph 3 involve parallelism and contrast.
7. What is the significance of these two questions in relation to Mill's assumptions in his argument?
8. Explain the effectiveness of the several infinitives in sentence 3 of paragraph 4.
9. Many of Mill's sentences are quite long. What is the effect of the several shorter sentences in paragraph 5?

DICTION

1. Look up *discrimination, animating, aliment, encroaching, acquiesce, latitude, despotism, professes, injunction, obstruction, gainsaid*.
2. To what extent do the following terms of Mill's arouse feelings in the reader—and what feelings? *ape-like, salt of the earth, stagnant pool, like cattle, dead matter, Niagara River, Dutch canal*.
3. How does Mill's discussion gain from the connotations of such terms as *machine, automaton, tree, living thing*?
4. Note some of Mill's metaphors, such as *cultivating, dulls and blunts* (par. 2), *preserve the soil, moulds, fetters* (par. 4), and try replacing them with non-metaphorical terms. What is the effect? Gain? Loss?
5. *Ex vi termini* means by force of the term.
6. Compare Mill's style with that of Madison. Which is the more formal, the more lively, the more serious, the more dignified, the more emotional, the more intellectual, the more realistic, the more concrete, the more complex, the more demanding?

ASSIGNMENT

Just as some people do not really wish to give to others the liberty that will allow them to develop in their individual ways, so some people criticize and grumble about certain institutions and concepts. Write an argument similar to Mill's to defend one of these institutions or concepts against those who "think that they can do very well without it." One might write on the value of:

1. Tradition
2. Higher education
3. The family
4. Religion
5. The sovereignty of the Federal Government
6. A system of taxation for society
7. Beauty

LAW AS THE MEANS TO FREEDOM
by A. Delafield Smith

¹ We need to see what the true meaning and function of law is, not in terms of authority, which is so commonly mistaken for law, but in terms of the rule of law in the ideal sense as a guide and challenge to the human will.

² The best example of how law, in the ideal sense, works, how it evokes the sense of freedom and stimulates the individual is the survey of a game. Have you ever asked yourself why the participation in a game is so excellent a medium for self-expression and character development? This question is often superficially answered in terms of the rein given to the competitive instincts of the individual and his "zest" for conquest. But have you ever considered that here, in a game, and perhaps here alone, we human beings really do act almost completely under the aegis of law? That, rather than competition, is the real source of the game's restorative value for the human spirit. Analyze the process step by step and you must be convinced that this is the truth.

³ Your first step upon entering a game is the assumption of a distinct personality. You become clothed in a personality defined by the rules of the game. You assume a legal or game personality. You may describe yourself as a first baseman, as a right guard, or as a dealer. But however you describe yourself you will see that what you have described is a legal status—one of the focal points in a legal pattern with rights and obligations suitable to the position. These rights and duties are defined by the rules under whose empery you have thus put both yourself and all

From *The Right to Life* by A. Delafield Smith (Chapel Hill, N.C., The University of North Carolina Press, 1955).

others with whom you have dealings. Your status, your rights, your obligations, all are secure, for the rules of the game are almost sure to be followed. The game indeed is defined by its rules. These are purely abstract. They are wholly free of will and dictation. They are pure rules of action composed usually in some physical setting which they serve to interpret and fashion till it becomes an arena of human action, just as, for example, the rules of the highway, in relation to the highway pattern itself, provide individuals with an arena on which they can operate successfully. Now the rules of the game have many functions. They, in fact, define the very goals that the players seek. One wins only in the context of the rules of the game. They determine inexorably the consequences of the player's action, every play that he makes. He acts solely in relation to the rules. Their empery is accepted like a fact or a circumstance. Finally, they challenge and stimulate him for he uses the rules to win. The game is otherwise unmanaged. An umpire or a referee is but an interpreter of the rules. He *can* be wrong. Such is the conception. This, then, may furnish an introduction to the real function of law in society.

⁴   Law gave birth to the concept of freedom. True it is that you can have no security in a situation in which every person and everything around you acts capriciously, unpredictably, or, in other words, lawlessly; but the point I wish to make is that while you would have no security in such an environment, it is more significant that you would have no freedom in such an environment. The reason you could not be free in such a situation is that you could not get anywhere you wanted to go or successfully do anything you wanted to do. You could make no plan in the expectation of carrying it out. You cannot possibly carry out any aim or goal of your own unless you have some basis for calculating what results may follow from any given act or activity of your own. Unless you can determine in advance what are the prospects and limitations of a given course of behavior, you cannot act intelligently. Whatever intelligence you may have will do you no good. You cannot adjust your own step to anyone else's step nor can you relate your conduct to any series of events or occurrences outside yourself except to the extent that they follow a pattern that you can learn about in advance of your action.

⁵   The only way to promote freedom is to devise a set of rules and thus construct a pattern which the various members of that society can follow. Each can then determine his own acts in the light of his knowledge of the rules. On this basis each can predict his field of action in advance and what results are likely to ensue from his acts; and so he gains freedom to plan and to carry out his plans. The more you attempt to administer society, however, the less free it becomes. There is opportunity for freedom of choice only in acting subject to the rules, and then only if the rules are freed of any element of will or dictation. If these rules are just rules that tell you what method or act will yield what results, like the rules of a game, you can then freely determine your own play. You can use the rules to win the game. The more abstract and objective the rule, the freer is the individual in the choice of his alternatives. The rules must be so written as to cover every possible eventuality of choice and action.

Study Questions

ORGANIZATION AND CONTENT

1. The assignment which Mr. Smith gave himself may look quite difficult: to convince people, most of whom have probably thought of law in terms of restriction, that law is the means to freedom; many people would think this a paradoxical idea. Mr. Smith approaches this challenging assignment by means of an analogy. In which sentence does he announce that he is going to make use of the analogy?
2. Paragraph 1 has what function?
3. In order to "clear the ground," what false idea does the author try to eliminate in paragraph 2?
4. What is he ready to do in paragraph 3?
5. Paragraph 3 has more than 20 sentences. To what are they devoted?
6. Which sentence is the topic sentence of paragraph 3? Why does the author mention the "rules of the highway"?
7. Explain the analogy used by Mr. Smith. Does his analogy hold? Are there important likenesses between the analogy and the situation he is discussing? Are there any significant differences?
8. How important is this analogy to his argument?

9. What idea essential to the argument is brought out in paragraph 4?
10. Does paragraph 4 have any connection with the analogy?
11. Is the first sentence of paragraph 5 a conclusion drawn from the preceding discussion, or is it simply an assertion of the proposition that the author is trying to prove?
12. On what evidence is he justified in saying "The more abstract and objective the rule, the freer is the individual in the choice of his alternatives"?
13. He also says in paragraph 5, "The more you attempt to administer society, . . . the less free it becomes." Is this idea brought out in, or covered by, the analogy?
14. Contrast Smith's argument with Madison's in regard to methods used.

SENTENCE STRUCTURE

1. Many of the sentences of this selection are addressed to "you." Why? What is the effect of thus addressing the reader? Is there any advantage for the author in doing so?
2. Indicate how repetition of certain terms supplies transition in paragraphs 3 and 4.
3. Compare Mr. Smith's sentence style with that of John Stuart Mill. Which is the more formal, the more lively, the more dignified, the more concrete, the more emotional, the more complex, the more demanding?

DICTION

1. Look up *aegis, assumption, empery, abstract, arena, context, inexorably, administer, objective, eventuality.*
2. Both Mr. Smith and James Madison were trained as lawyers. Compare their arguments to answer the question: To what extent has their legal training influenced their choice of diction?

ASSIGNMENT

Write an argument in which you, like Mr. Smith, use an analogy. Some suggestions are:

1. Education should be carefully controlled; teachers should know exactly what operation to perform day by day (for educating a person is like turning out a product in a factory).
2. Education is best when students have much freedom (for

education is like the growth of a tree; all the tree needs is a chance at things that are good for it, without unnecessary obstacles).

3. Students should have (or not have) freedom in choosing courses (for a college is like a great city with a wealth of things and experiences at the disposal of the inhabitants).

4. Students should have freedom in choosing courses (for studying some subject that one dislikes is like climbing a mountain).

5. It is good (or not good) to make oneself into a sophisticated person (for doing so is like baking and decorating a cake, or trimming a Christmas tree).

6. We should encourage more discipline in every phase of our society (for in Japanese flower-arranging, effects of grace and simplicity are obtained by disciplined training; or, as Alexander Pope wrote:

> True ease in writing comes from art, not chance,
> As those move easiest who have learned to dance.)

7. No politician can be a completely good man; a politician should be prepared to have to make compromises and even to do some things that he knows are not good, in order to be able to accomplish the good things that he regards as most important (for a basketball player though committing many fouls may make enough goals to insure that his team will win).

RELIGION IS IMPORTANT FOR MAN'S SURVIVAL NOW *by Lewis Mumford*

Not the least important force we must mobilize, in the interests of survival, is an ancient one: that of religion. Both Benjamin Kidd a generation ago, and Henri Bergson in our own time, interpreted religion as a self-preservative effort, on the part of life, to guard man against the discouraging effects of his own achievements in knowledge. There is a profound truth in these interpretations. Though most of the classic religions have dwelled on the familiar facts of man's limitations and frustrations, cen-

From *Values of Survival*, copyright 1946, by Lewis Mumford. Reprinted by permission of Harcourt, Brace & World, Inc.

tered in the ultimate mystery of death, they have all guarded life itself, as zealously as the vestals guarded fire. Hinduism, Confucianism, Buddhism, Judaism, Christianity, even Mohammedanism, have sought to curb man's impulses to destruction and disintegration: each of them interdicts random killing, each of them encourages procreation, each of them has sought to foster love.

2   In this moment of common peril, we should do well to overlook the hypocrisies and failures of the orthodox: their very superstitions have nevertheless kept the ignorant, the willful, and the destructive under some limited sense of order and some minimum system of control. If the symbols of religion do not always stand up under rational examination, if their myths are more mysterious than the mysteries they would explain, that is not necessarily a proof of their inability to penetrate and control the irrational elements in man. Religion's function, in fact, is to redress man's pride in his intellect, to reduce his conceit and his complacence, so that he will be better fortified to face the ordeal of reality. Mankind is a-float on a frail life-raft. Religion understands the monsters of the deep and the storms that come up in the night.

3   Religion reminds man of his creatureliness and his creativeness, his impotence and his power, his cosmic littleness and his cosmic preciousness—for the tiny spark of consciousness man carries in his soul may be, up to now, the final event toward which the so-called physical universe has moved. Religion's cosmic time sense, achieved long before astronomy sustained the intuition with exact calculations, is a brake against the possibility that man might sacrifice his own long future to some temporary gratification or some temporary triumph. Here is a latent power for man's self-preservation: on the whole, theologians have made a more prompt response to the atomic bomb than any other group except the atomic physicists themselves, though they have still to show the capacity for unified effort that will make a wider renewal possible.

4   Morality is Sancho Panza to religion's Don Quixote; for morality develops out of the customs of the tribe and those customs, too, are usually life-preservative ones, though they may clash with those of other tribes. Modern man, proud of his fearless investigation of every part of the universe, conscious of his

increasing powers to control his circumstances, has shown something less than forbearance to those primitive cultures whose daily acts are limited by taboos. But in throwing off the irrational object of most taboos, modern man has also forfeited the very habit of inhibition that the taboo imposed. He has thus forgotten one of the most essential secrets of man's advance: the practice of restraint. Whereas the older midbrain is the seat of man's instinctual energies and his explosive emotions, the newer forebrain, which takes care of his higher behavior, is also the seat of his inhibitions. Without the development of these inhibitions man's untempered curiosity might, long before this, have proved suicidal.

⁵ In little matters, modern man acknowledges taboos: he does not spit in a subway car, blow his nose in public without using a handkerchief, or enter a house with a quarantine notice posted on its door. But in general, his plan of life has resulted, not in exchanging taboos for rational restraints, but in exchanging taboos for equally irrational habits of relaxation. For the last two hundred years a long succession of thinkers, from Diderot and Rousseau onward, have urged man to throw off his ancient taboos: to act on his impulses, yield to his desires, abandon measure in his gratifications. If man were wholly rational and wholly good, these counsels would perhaps have been profitable: but Dostoyevsky, who understood the demonic in man, pointed out long ago the dangers of this moral nihilism; and in our day those dangers have assumed cosmic dimensions.

⁶ Morality, in the elementary form of accepted inhibitions, is the first step toward the conscious control of the powers man now commands: without this lowest form of morality, engrained in habit, no higher form can be practiced. What Irving Babbitt called the inner check—the vital restraint—is essential to our survival. Promptly we must reverse Blake's dictum—we must bless braces and damn relaxes.

⁷ This moral tightening of the bit comes very hard to modern man; for it is no exaggeration to say that he has attempted in the past generation to live by the pleasure principle: he has tried to establish a regime of limitless gratifications without accepting deprivations or penalties. The very quantification of life through machine production has lifted many natural limits that once pre-

vailed. So self-indulgent have we become that even a temporary shortage of cigarettes in America evoked a response far more irrational in character than any religious taboo on smoking would be: in the midst of a biting blizzard, crowds waited in line for a whole hour in order to purchase their quota of cigarettes. The indecent haste with which the American Government threw off the rationing of foods after the Japanese surrender, at a time when the rest of the war-battered world was close to starvation, is an indication of a popular unwillingness to exercise self-control: an unwillingness most prevalent in the very circles that exercise most political influence.

8 Morally, such people are as unfit for the control of atomic power as a chronic alcoholic would be for the inheritance of a vast stock of whiskey. Those who have lost respect for taboos of any kind are most in need of their self-preservative principle.

9 Now, experience demands that we should recognize the place of negative stimuli in human development. Pains, abstentions, renunciations, inhibitions, are perhaps as essential for human development as more positive nurture. During the war, fighting men learned this lesson; it gave them power to confront danger and surmount it; and where civilians were placed under the same stresses, as in cities that endured aerial bombardment, they learned the same hard lesson. The imaginative widening of this experience among people who are still unchastened is an essential measure. To recover the very habit of restraint, to subject every act to measure, to place limits even on goods that may be offered in limitless quantities—this is the communal response we must make to the challenge of both physical and moral disintegration. The very processes of democracy, which it is so essential to extend to world organization, demand a high degree of conscious moderation. That is possibly why the most restrained of peoples, the English, are also the best exemplars of democratic processes. Every civilian must master, as the price of society's survival, the lesson that military organization teaches the soldier: group survival requires the acceptance of sacrifice.

Study Questions

ORGANIZATION AND CONTENT

1. What constructive aspect of religion is emphasized in paragraph 1?
2. Does paragraph 2 indicate that Mumford approves of religious superstitions?
3. According to paragraphs 1 and 2, what is the relation between religion and intellect and knowledge?
4. Sentence 1 of paragraph 3 stresses certain contrasts. What do these contrasts and "religion's cosmic time sense" have to do with man's survival?
5. Interpret the metaphor involving the idealistic knight Don Quixote and his fat, earthy squire Sancho Panza. According to paragraph 4, how has science tended to weaken morality?
6. Are the acknowledged "taboos" mentioned in paragraph 5 really rational restraints? If they are, does this fact affect Mumford's argument in any way?
7. Why does Mumford believe that the counsels of such men as Diderot, Rousseau, and William Blake have not been profitable?
8. Does Mumford exaggerate when he asserts that the dangers of moral nihilism have now assumed *cosmic* dimensions?
9. Paragraph 6 emphasizes the "lowest form of morality"; of what value is it in the argument?
10. What difficulties are represented by machine production and the pleasure principle?
11. Why is paragraph 8 so short? What issue in the argument does this paragraph deal with?
12. In paragraph 9 in what way are "people who are still unchastened" to be paralleled with fighting men and civilians?
13. What do the English people exemplify in this paragraph?
14. State Mumford's argument so as to bring out the logical connections among the points.
15. List the issues of his argument.

SENTENCE STRUCTURE

1. In every paragraph except paragraph 8 there is at least one sentence with a colon; paragraph 7 has three such sentences. For what purpose are the colons used?

2. Does this regular use of the colon constitute a mannerism of style in Mumford's work?
3. In terms of structure what does sentence 5 of paragraph 1 have in common with sentence 1 of paragraph 2?
4. Does Mumford repeat ideas (using parallel grammatical elements) more than is necessary? (Consider sentences 2 and 3 of paragraph 2, sentence 1 of paragraph 3, sentences 2 and 5 of paragraph 9.)
5. To what extent does Mumford interrupt his sentences to place parenthetical material in the middle—as in sentence 2 of paragraph 1, sentence 2 of paragraph 3, sentence 2 of paragraph 4?
6. Which sentences in paragraphs 1, 2, and 4 are shortest? What is the effect of these short sentences?
7. Classify the sentences of each paragraph according to whether they begin with subjects or with dependent material. Are there too many sentences of either kind in any paragraph?
8. Does Mumford write with sufficient variety of sentence structure, or not?

DICTION

1. Look up *mobilize, vestals, interdict, hypocrisy, irrational, impotence, cosmic, intuition, latent, theologians, morality, inhibition, measure, nihilism, quantification, unchastened.*
2. From what languages do these words come?
3. Do some research on the men to whom Mumford alludes.
4. Note the connotations of certain terms: "frail life-raft," "monsters of the deep," in paragraph 2, "tightening of the bit" in paragraph 7. What do these metaphors accomplish in the argument?
5. Is Mumford's vocabulary prevailingly abstract or concrete?
6. How are *creatureliness* and *creativeness* related in their origin? How do they contrast in their meanings?

ASSIGNMENT

You may wish to take issue with Mumford; there are various questions which might be raised and which might be developed into counterarguments—for example:

1. Is it not true that human beings are wicked and that every man has his price? Therefore, such efforts as Mumford advises are doomed to failure.
2. Considering the worldliness of modern religion—how women dress up for church and how much emphasis is put on recrea-

tion in church activities—is it true that religion has retained its alleged powers for good?

3. Considering the great emphasis on money raising in churches, is it not true that modern religion has become too commercialized to be an effective curb upon man's desires and powers?

4. Would it be honest to favor religion only for a special benefit it may provide, meanwhile overlooking "the hypocrisies and failures of the orthodox"?

5. Mumford mentions several different religions in paragraph 1. If you have special knowledge of some of these, you might argue that one of them has a greater power than the others for Mumford's purposes.

6. If you are less willing than Mumford to ignore the rational inadequacy of religious symbols, you might argue that the study of the classics and of philosophy has equal value with religion for developing moderation and control of instinctual impulses.

INDEX OF AUTHORS